Bound
To Be
Free

Bound To Be Free

Richard B. McKenzie

HOOVER INSTITUTION PRESS
Stanford University
Stanford, California

The Hoover Institution on War, Revolution and Peace, founded at Stanford University in 1919 by the late President Herbert Hoover, is an interdisciplinary research center for advanced study on domestic and international affairs in the twentieth century. The views expressed in its publications are entirely those of the authors and do not necessarily reflect the views of the staff, officers, or Board of Overseers of the Hoover Institution.

Hoover Press Publication 255

International Standard Book Number: 0-8179-7551-9
Library of Congress Catalog Card Number: 81-81402
Printed in the United States of America

Design by P. Kelley Baker

To
Professor James M. Buchanan

In Memory of
Ethel B. McKenzie

Contents

Preface   ix

1 The Crosscurrents of Social Politics   1

2 Government as the Problem, Not the
Answer   13

3 The Primacy of the Individual   47

4 The Collectivist Mentality   75

5 The Social Nexus:
Free Enterprise and the Constitution   95

6 "The Governmental Habit"   125

7 The Dynamic Duo:
Free Speech and Free Markets   143

8 The Return to a Free Economy   159

Notes   175
Bibliography   189
Index   195

FROM THE LETTERS OF LORD MACAULAY

Holly Lodge, Kensington
London, May 23d, 1857

Dear Sir:

I have long been convinced that institutions purely democratic must, sooner or later, destroy liberty, or civilization, or both . . .

It is quite plain that your government will never be able to restrain a distressed and discontented majority. For with you the majority is the government, and has the rich, who are always a minority, absolutely at its mercy. The day will come, when in the State of New York a multitude of people, none of whom have had more than half a breakfast, or expect to have more than half a dinner, will choose a legislature. Is it possible to doubt what sort of legislature will be chosen? On one side is the statesman preaching patience, respect for vested rights, strict obedience of public faith. On the other is a demagogue ranting about the tyranny of capitalists and usurers, and asking why anybody should be permitted to drink champagne and to ride in a carriage. Which of the two candidates is likely to be preferred by a working man?

I seriously apprehend that you will, in some such season of adversity as I have described, do things which will prevent prosperity from returning; that you will act as people would in a year of scarcity, devour all of the seedcorn and thus make the next year, a year not of scarcity but of absolute famine. There will be, I fear, spoilation. The spoilation will increase the distress. The distress will produce fresh spoilation. There is nothing to stay you. Your Constitution is all sail and no anchor.

As I said before, when a society has entered on this downward progress, either civilization or liberty must perish. Either some Caesar or Napoleon will seize the reins of government with a strong hand; or your republic will be as fearfully plundered and laid waste in the twentieth century as the Roman Empire was by barbarians who came from without, and that your Huns and Vandals will have been engendered within your country by your own institutions.

Thomas Babington Macaulay

Preface

This book is ostensibly about economics—about the economy and how it is and should be organized in a society that treasures individual freedom. Its message, however, transcends the boundaries of economic science as normally conceived—namely, over the years we must all live by principles based on ultimate values that guide and take the worry out of the day-to-day decisions we must make. Otherwise, we can fall victim to our own passing whims and fancies and lose our sense of purpose and direction.

This message is no less applicable to the consideration of public policies than it is to our personal lives. We select personal principles of behavior fully aware that our actions in and reactions to complex social events (which, because of their immediacy, can rarely be fully appreciated at the time) will be held in check. We willingly constrain ourselves because our view is to the future—to the long run and the outcome, on balance, of a whole series of social events of which we are a part.

Similarly, in devising a social structure for a free people, we must seek guiding but constraining principles. Without such transcending principles, we can become confused by a bewildering array of public policies that have no unifying theme—that are offered for legislative consideration by every conceivable interest group that believes its cause deserves special attention from government.

Somewhat paradoxically, freedom—including economic freedom—ultimately spells limits on what we and others can do. This book is a search for the guiding but constraining principles for government

---

Opposite Page: The distinguished nineteenth-century English historian was writing to Henry Stephens Randall, author of *Life of Thomas Jefferson*.

and, thereby, for ourselves and others. Constraints on government are ultimately restrictions on what we—businessmen and social reformers alike—can do through the use of governmental powers. These curbs can, however, give each of us a measure of freedom, both economic and political, by denying unchecked powers to some through the use of an unchecked government. In short, this book is a search for the constitutional principles that must undergird a free economy; it is, therefore, necessarily a search for the principles of a constrained government.

Lord Macaulay's observation, in the letter that opens this book, that in an unconstrained democracy poor people may appropriate the wealth of the rich through their voting powers, was very insightful. He failed to see, however, that open-ended democratic rule does not always mean majority rule—it can mean minority rule. Special interest groups of all persuasions, including the poor *and* the rich, may exploit their political power to pursue narrowly conceived goals. The end result may well be, as it has been, that government expends much of its scarce energies shifting the nation's income back and forth among competing groups in response to ever-changing political winds.

If men and women were angels, to paraphrase James Madison, government would be unnecessary. But they are not angels, and in framing a government that is to be administered by passionate, real-world people, "the great difficulty lies in this: You must first enable the government to control the governed; and in the next place, oblige it to control itself." Constitutional principles are social inventions designed to contain government in order that we, as a nation, can avoid the sorry end-state in which political competition for the use of government power is, on balance, destructive of productive incentives and, consequently, destructive of the general good. Indeed, one of my purposes in this book is to show that without constitutional constraints on government, free enterprise contains its own internal contradiction.

The book has been something of a labor of love. It has given me an opportunity to take a broad view and to write analytically about the long-term structure of the economy. The reader is, however, likely to sense that my heart is where my analysis is. Unabashedly, I write with a sense of urgency, recognizing that general issues in political economy, like those considered here, have both moral and analytical foundations. There has probably never been a better time during this century to reconsider the relationship between the market and the political system and between economic and political freedoms—that is, between constitutional government and the free enterprise system.

My work is, of course, founded on the ideas and writings of many friends, teachers, and colleagues who have, over the years, discussed with me the necessary constitutional foundations of a free society. Although I cannot hope to thank each of them, I must express my appreciation to several people who read all or a portion of the manuscript and made many valuable suggestions: Hugh Macaulay, Rex Cottle, Gene Uselton, Delores Martin, Louis Spadaro, Melvin McKenzie, Russell Shannon, Bruce Yandle, George Uhimchuk, and Holley Ulbrich. Ann Wortham's very careful reading of the manuscript was particularly valuable; she repeatedly reminded me of what it means to be "free and different, which is to be human."

For the past four years, I have been very fortunate to be able to call the members of my department at Clemson University my colleagues. Over numerous cups of coffee, the ideas contained in this book have, unknown to many of them, been tested, retested, and developed into a coherent pattern. Without their willingness to hear me out and their support, this book literally could never have been written.

I am especially indebted to James M. Buchanan at the Center for the Study of Public Choice, Virginia Polytechnic Institute and State University, for the considerable advice, encouragement, and direction he gave me during the preparation of this book. Because I have been a student of his, have read so much of what he has written, and have over the years spent many hours discussing with him the relationship between constitutions and markets, every chapter of this book reflects his influence. For these reasons, I am honored to be able to dedicate this book to him.

I am also grateful to Mary Ann McKenzie for making valuable substantive comments and giving editorial assistance; to Jill Williams and Betsy Gourlay for typing and retyping the initial drafts of the manuscript; and to Karen Lea Jones for computerizing the final draft. All of these people must know that my appreciation for their generous help is heartfelt. Finally, I am indebted to the Institute for Humane Studies, the J. R. Sirrine Foundation, and the Hoover Institution on War, Revolution and Peace for the financial support they afforded me. Portions of the book were previously published in substantially different form by the International Institute for Economic Research, Council for a Competitive Economy, and the Fiscal Policy Council.

Bound
To Be
Free

The
Crosscurrents
of
Social Politics

We hold these truths to be self-evident; that all men are created equal; that they are endowed by their Creator with certain unalienable rights; that among these are life, liberty and the pursuit of happiness.

Thomas Jefferson
Declaration of Independence

CHAPTER 1

Thomas Jefferson was no common man, and in the words he wrote he left us no common legacy. But if modern experience demonstrates anything, the truths that Jefferson declared to be self-evident are not that at all. Individual freedom is under attack from all flanks in the name of "social reform;" government has grown and continues to grow like a social cancer; "free enterprise" has become a four-letter word used only cautiously by its defenders.

Far from being self-evident, the basic values of equality before the law, liberty, and the pursuit of happiness must be asserted and reasserted and nurtured by honest discussion of their importance to the course of human events and of means of protecting them from erosion. In one respect, this book provides a restatement of the philosophical underpinnings of a free society; it is, in a way, a trip into the mind of Jefferson and what he stood for. In another, it has a practical objective: to explain our present economic predicament (satisfying to no one, not even advocates of expanded government) and to search for ways of protecting, as best we can by constitutional means, a relatively free economy—that is, the free enterprise system. That search necessarily begins with an appraisal of current constraints on government and necessarily ends with practical constitutional remedies.

A free economy is a problem in constitutional government. Freedom of enterprise is, however, only one of many interrelated freedoms that must ultimately be defended as a basic value and by strict constitutional bounds on government. One theme of this book is that *the case for a free economy is largely a case for freedom in general*. The search for a free economy, therefore, begins with some reflections on the confusing crosscurrents of social politics relating to freedom observed in recent decades.

"FREE AT LAST!"

The 1960s and 1970s were decades of far-reaching social unrest and change, of dramatic social contradictions that in no small way tested the fabric of American society. Martin Luther King, echoing the emotions of a whole race, declared from the steps of the Lincoln Memorial, "Free at last, free at last . . . thank God Almighty, free at last!" He had gone to the top of the mountain and had, within a relatively short time, seen many vestiges of a feudal cultural and legal system fall in the name of individual dignity and freedom. And he had seen over the mountain into a future in which people would be judged not by class traits or skin color but by individual merit and action.

Martin Luther King was a social reformer. Although his efforts were sometimes misguided, he was a Jeffersonian dreamer in many respects, a throwback to the formative era of the American political system when the pursuit of life and liberty at the individual level was the standard for judging social action. King, and the movement he represented, was a contradiction: he was an activist with collectivist tendencies, but he was an individualist inspired by the hallmarks of freedom he articulated so well. Such contradictions, however, peppered much social commentary of his time, and we are left to wonder why.

Choruses of "We Shall Overcome" were still being heard when nightly newscasts of the 1960s vividly portrayed the unconventional and seemingly uncorked life-styles of the "flower children," "hippies," and "yippies." Many of them were antiestablishment, anticapitalist, antiwar, antiparents, antilaw—anti just about anything smacking of social regimentation. Defiance of convention was their theme. Many dared passersby and those who sought to understand them to object to what they were doing or to offer advice on how they should live, and they often scoffed at anyone accepting their challenge. The five-pointed marijuana leaf was their unifying banner for collective action. They wanted to "find themselves" by taking "trips" on various drugs, which by their nature were solitary ventures into the subconscious and the unconscious. They questioned, even denied, the validity of any social system, but they formed "families" and communes. They mocked capitalists and the system capitalists represented while they depended on and even lived off that system. They were self-proclaimed individualists who wanted "to do their own thing," but they were none-too-obvious conformists in pursuit of nonconformity. They were sometimes hell-bent on violating society's rules of reasonable conduct, but many were avid supporters of extensions of the welfare state.

MORE BANNERS

Reverend King's memorable words seemed to open a floodgate of protests by groups who felt that they had been oppressed by social norms and rules and deserved "liberation." A whole generation of young people, detecting an individual and moral principle at stake in a war that no one wanted to win or had the guts to lose, shouted to the country, "Hell no, We won't go!"

The 1960s and 1970s saw the banners of Women's Liberation, Gay Liberation, Black Power, Gray Power, Brown Power, and even Secretarial Power raised so often that many who sat back and observed the passing demonstrations could only question where the parade was going—if anywhere. They could only wonder if the system—any system—could survive continual attacks from all flanks. Each group felt oppressed by "society" but sought "justice" by appealing to "social consciousness" and "social responsibility" and "social reform," which generally meant the development of new laws and new programs to protect the protesting group. In a sense, the problem (the denial of individuality) was often seen to be the solution. The question that begs for an answer is, again, Why?

THE EDUCATION PARADOX

Businesses during the 1960s and 1970s mounted advertising campaigns intended to illustrate what "free enterprise means to you" and donated considerable sums to universities for chairs and institutes of free enterprise. Executives gave freely of their time, effort, and financial resources to local and national movements proposing to educate the masses on the virtues of the market system and to overcome their "economic illiteracy." In a 1962 manifesto on economic education, the Committee for Economic Development (an organization supported by large businesses) declared:

Economic literacy is vital to the survival of the American Society.

Our human freedoms, as reflected in our democratic form of government, depend upon the decision making of millions of individual citizens. Our living standard, so long the envy of other peoples, can grow no faster than the soundness of the economic decisions made by our people. Finally, our ability to meet our obligations abroad and to defend ourselves rests to a large degree on economic wisdom at home.

Today we find ourselves and our system challenged on every level . . . Evidence mounts that we have failed to train many of our people for this broad responsibility.[1]

With few changes in wording, the same battle cry would be equally, if not more, applicable to the educational deficiency of the public in the 1980s. Musing over the forces affecting the educational and ideological foundations of the American system, former Treasury Secretary William Simon thinks that our problems are more fundamental.

Too many Americans, particularly pro–free enterprise conservatives, have assumed an immense intelligence in the liberal world and have concluded that when liberals destroyed U.S. production, they knew what they were doing, i.e., that they were guilty of a conspiracy. They were not conspirators; they were intellectual basket cases in the realm of basic economics. It takes an immense resistance to logic and fact not to know that one cannot simultaneously control prices, inflate costs, ban production, increase taxes, grant counterproductive subsidies—and expect healthy, vigorous production to result. Amy Carter [President Jimmy Carter's daughter] could understand perfectly well what was wrong with such a system if her father regulated her lemonade stand the way the liberals in Congress have regulated the energy industry.[2]

Perhaps Simon is right. The efforts of the business and educational communities to improve the public's economic literacy, however, have been meager compared to the immensity of the task at hand. At best, business people, economists, and social philosophers interested in "doing something" (almost anything) have been tilting at a windmill that has barely been slowed, much less reversed. If reissued today, the battle cry of economic education would, no doubt, be tempered by sober reflection on the years of effort that have been overwhelmed by the volume of issues placed in and settled by public forums. As Walter Wriston, chairman of Citicorp, writes:

> In America today, only the rich or the very poor have any possibility whatsoever of learning what the law is, surely a precondition to voluntary conformity. It is becoming increasingly true that the great bulk of our population has to ignore the law completely to survive. There are so many laws and regulations with the force of law, that it is a fair bet that everyone is now in violation of some statute—we just do not know which one. Not only do we not know what the law is, but we cannot afford to find out.[3]

As citizens, we are asked to appraise a growing list of issues about which we understand little. Can a coherent national policy ever be achieved when the citizenry is so poorly prepared to comprehend the day-to-day flow of new policies, new laws, and new regulations?

THE VOTING DILEMMA

The contradictions of current social policies are nowhere more apparent than in the willingness of people to vote. An ever-growing variety of complex economic issues is being settled by collective decision, but fewer and fewer people are sufficiently interested in politics to vote, much less to investigate the issues or to understand the effects of policy changes on the efficiency, equity, and stability of the social system. In 1960 more than 60 percent of the voting age population participated in the Kennedy-Nixon presidential election; by 1980, in an election that at the time the polls opened was characterized as "too close to call" and "a real horse race," the percentage of eligible voters who took the trouble to go to the polls had declined to less than 54 percent, continuing a trend under way for decades. In a typical off-year congressional election, 60 percent of the voting age public does not exercise its basic franchise. In local elections sometimes as few as 10 percent of the people determine who controls local government, which may be taking a growing share of community resources.

Most voters know precious little about the issues at stake or candidates' position on those issues. Voters cannot be well informed given the great number of complex issues now stuffed into political debates.

At some point the political system, which we seem to be treating as a "free good," will surely short-circuit from the demands placed on it.

SOCIAL CONTRADICTIONS AND CONSTITUTIONAL ANARCHY

Historians of the future will probably view the 1960s and 1970s as a major turning point in American social and legal history. The nature of this juncture is difficult to specify because the relative strengths of the conflicting sociopolitical crosscurrents are not yet clear. We must, from the perspective of the early 1980s, still wonder what many of those currents mean and where they are going. It is clearly possible that the United States will continue to follow Great Britain down the "yellow brick road" of collectivism. On the other hand, there are small but important signs of hope. The expansion of government may be checked and possibly reversed by more Proposition 13s. There may be others like California's tax slasher Howard Jarvis who are waiting a chance to stand up and proclaim to the world, as did the TV anchorman in the movie *Network*, "I'm mad as hell! And I'm not going to take it any longer." Although growth in the federal government has not been reversed, the Reagan administration, during its first year in office, displayed a rare dedication to controlling the expansion of government.

Although we cannot know what changes lie ahead, we do know that we have witnessed many instances of social schizophrenia. Persons concerned with racial discrimination, for example, have sought to break down legal and social obstructions that force individuals to be judged as members of groups; but many of these same persons have thought nothing of using race as an arbitrary social classification in an attempt to redress damage done in past generations—to try to redo what cannot be redone. Others who acknowledge the importance of the individual and espouse the ideals of individualism have been enamored of sociological "scientism," which, almost by habit, employs sex, income, education, location, intelligence, and political associations, as well as race, as strategic variables to explain social ills and to suggest remedies. The inconsistency of the avowed individualist who seeks social reform through piecemeal government policy can be understood, if not excused, by the necessity of making reforms manageable through the use of groups and classes. (None would be so arrogant as to think that he could reform society by seeking remedies for the social ills faced by each individual.) Consistency, however, has not been a guiding principle behind many reform movements.

Then there are the many businessmen and women who pay lip service to free enterprise, but, as discussed in some detail later, often make Washington their second headquarters. Free traders have often pleaded with Congress for import tariffs, protective regulations, sub-sidies, and restrictions on entry into *their* markets. The very people who decry growth in federal and state budgets have often lobbied for an expansion of government expenditures affecting their industry, or better, their particular business. Indeed, it is not unreasonable to speculate that businesses during the 1960s and 1970s spent far more money to secure government favors—at the expense of the taxpaying public—than to articulate the virtues of capitalism. The principles of free enterprise have, almost as a matter of course, given way to the government "bail-out."

"Government of the people, by the people, for the people," has become a competitive struggle among businesses for political influence. The bottom line of this competition is economic profit and, at times, economic survival. In the knowledge that principle can easily succumb to political competition, politicians have come to enjoy and to prosper from their expanded role as auctioneers of political favors. Free enter-prise is not dead. Its arena of action has simply shifted from the market to the political system, from a positive-sum game of market production to a negative-sum game of government redistribution.

During the 1960s and 1970s, people called for—nay, demanded— egalitarianism and freedom, consumer protection and individualism, growth in government and protection of human rights, individual opportunity and social security, scarcely realizing the contradictions implicit in each of these demands. People wanted "law and order," but the Constitution was so fractured by a sequence of dismantling court cases that it was a rare instance of government intervention in the market that could be held to violate constitutional precepts. Even liberal legal scholars, like Raoul Berger from Harvard, have lamented the breakdown of constitutional constraints on the judiciary.[4]

In the 1960s and 1970s, the United States was not a constitutional democracy in the sense that it was guided and directed by, to use Nobel laureate Friedrich Hayek's phrase, "just rules of conduct" embodied in a document to which people ascribed in practice as well as in principle. The "rule of expediency" has now effectively replaced the "rule of law;" each social ill is judged on its own merits, not as one in a sequence of events over time that must be dealt with by broad principles of what is and is not permissible.

To be sure, the United States is a democracy in the sense that votes are taken (on just about anything), but it is a democracy unconstrained by set boundaries of legitimate collective action. Legitimacy is now determined, not by principle but by the possession of the necessary votes. In such an environment, no one should be surprised to find politics becoming a circus of revolving majorities and special interest groups. In short, by the late 1970s, the United States had become, in political economist James Buchanan's words, a "constitutional anarchy."[5]

ANSWERS AND MORE ANSWERS

Why the contradictions and the crosscurrents? The easy answer is that we are all nuts, intent on destroying the social and economic system that has nourished us; that we have lost the faith and no longer hold certain truths as self-evident or view the pursuit of life, liberty, and individual happiness as unalienable rights; that our moral character has been warped, as predicted by the detractors of capitalism; and that we as a people no longer hold to the transcendent values necessary to sustain an open society. Perhaps social philosopher Wilhelm Ropke was correct when he argued in 1960 that the market is important in and of itself but much more is needed for its long-term survival:

> Self-discipline, a sense of justice, honesty, fairness, chivalry, mod-
> eration, public spirit, respect for human dignity, firm ethical
> norms—all of these are things which people must possess before they
> go to the market and compete with each other. These are the indis-
> pensable supports which preserve both market and competition from
> degeneration. Family, church, genuine communities, and tradition
> are their sources.[6]

Perhaps the very success of the market led to the loss of its moral substructure. Abundant casual evidence in the morning newspaper suggests that many of the values included in Ropke's list have lost their force in America, as well as in other parts of the world.

Accepting these answers, however, sidesteps the issue of why we have "all gone nuts," "lost the faith," and/or "degenerated into moral poverty." Is it due to a simple change in tastes and preferences; an expansion of technology; a restructuring of the genes; or that catchall explanation of sociologists, a change in the "social environment?" These reasons for observed social contradictions and crosscurrents may be worth pursuing. However, the overriding purpose of this study is to demonstrate the inextricable connection between free enterprise and constitutional government—that is, a system of just rules of conduct that constrains collective action over a sequence of historical and social events. Another purpose is to argue that free enterprise in the United States has collapsed to the extent it has because of the systematic dismantling of constitutional constraints on government. Further, once constitutional constraints on government are broken, free enterprise is destroyed from within, not from without. When constitutional barriers on government are torn down, free enterprise contracts not so much because of autonomous actions of a government that moves like the Blob over the economic landscape but because of the exploits of free enterprisers who seek to use unconstrained government to further their own interests. In the jargon of contemporary economics, unconstrained government induces entrepreneurs to become "rent seekers" through government. This is not a new argument; it was articulated by Adam Smith and others before him. But it is an argument that is in desperate need of modern restatement and reinterpretation.

In short, this study attempts to show if the connection between free enterprise and constitutional government can explain many of the apparent inconsistencies in modern social politics: for example, the social reformer who talks about individual freedom and seeks collective reform and the businessman who wants a free enterprise system but sits on the doorstep of government waiting for handouts. The analysis will draw on and synthesize the work of many people; but, it will, it is hoped, break new ground.

As individuals, we are able to understand more about our social context than we are able to explore and explain on a verbal level. We are able to sense basic concepts, fundamental rights, and the central issues of the social predicament with a clarity that eludes us when we try to talk or write about them. The inherent problem of verbalizing what we sense has been one of the most important, if not the most important, of the restrictions on the systematic development of the case for and moral necessity of the free market system. The importance of the issues at stake, however, demands that we make every effort to overcome the problems of communication. For too long, too many people with common interests in the health and welfare of the country's future but with different political perspectives have been talking at cross-purposes.

The social dilemma we face is relatively easy to define in general terms: we all want good laws and good government because of the social benefits they yield. However, there is an ever-present Catch 22. Individuals have little incentive to participate in the development of good laws and good government and to assent to them if they are established, even tentatively (a point developed in Chapter 5). The incentive to violate any constitutional form of government at the instant of its development is pervasive; so much so that we must wonder how any constitution, much less a "constitution of liberty," can be established. The critical question posed by this social dilemma, and addressed in this study, is If a constitution is a general statement of principles to be interpreted by men, how do we prevent the "rule of men" and foster the "rule of law"? As Felix Frankfurter observed, "People have been taught to believe that when the Supreme Court speaks it is not they [the justices] who speak but the Constitution, whereas, of course, in so many cases it is *they* who speak and *not* the Constitution."[7] The catch is so all-embracing that we must wonder how humanity ever took the first step out of the Hobbesian jungle in which there is no law and people are relentlessly engaged in combat. Explaining those first steps, and the necessity for them, is far more difficult than explaining why or how we have recently taken steps back toward the jungle.

There are those who hold that achieving constitutional government is simple: people should accept the authority of the Constitution and those who formed it.[8] This suggests that we, in effect, consult those who can tell us what authority is, where to find it, and how and to what extent to make use of it. Such explanations give the impression that the substance of authority, which gives vitality and staying power to constitutional law, can readily be found. The only problem is that we have little idea of what authority is, much less of how it can be determined. Furthermore, the implied solution to the social dilemma—the acceptance of authority—seems equivalent to a denial of the existence of the basic social dilemma: how to escape the jungle permanently. If individual assent to authority is all that is necessary to make "good" laws possible or to make good judges make good decisions about the good laws that are devised by good legislators, all of whom behave the way that they do because of the authority of the law, there is no problem. We should be able to step from the jungle with ease and to resist any movement back with equal ease. The concept of authority may be our last great hope of holding onto the remnants of a free market system, but it is difficult to accept an argument that maintains that the problem *is* the solution.

This study explicitly rejects the view of government that requires that government officials be good persons, or at least perfectible. Rather, it assumes imperfect real people who seek, through social agreement, a reasonable way out of the social dilemma they face. In searching for a free economy, this work starts with the presumption that people are good in the sense that they have a moral capacity and, within broad bounds, a commonality of interests in a stable and prosperous society. However, it also recognizes the limits of "goodness" and seeks institutions serving this commonality of interests within those limits.

In the final analysis, an argument for the resurrection of a free economy must attempt to convince others of the tolerable appropriateness of the free market system for an imperfect world, ruled by imperfect men. There is, unfortunately, no ironclad case for any set of social institutions. Each is defective to some extent. And we need not pretend otherwise. A sufficient argument for a free economy need be made only in terms of its superiority to other conceivable social systems.

Finally, the case for constitutional government is not an argument for a perfectly inflexible system incapable of changing with the pushes and tugs of developments over time. Rather, it is an argument for a predisposition in favor of constitutional rules that should be altered only when the evidence overwhelmingly supports the need for change. It is an argument for a predisposition in favor of individual as opposed to collective action, one that would shift the burden of proof for expansion in government *to* the shoulders of those who would throttle individual liberty. That is all that can be demanded of any case for a free economy, and all that is attempted here.

Government as the Problem, Not the Answer

Who can see what will come in the next two centuries any more clearly than our forefathers could envision what vast changes lay ahead in the two centuries just completed? In a way, our starting point is similar to theirs. Recall the traditional mercantalist controls of central government rejected by our Founders: the fixing of prices, wages, and interest rates; the outlawing of forestalling and engrossing; the regulating of the quality of goods; the licensing of labor; the chartering of corporations; and the establishment of state enterprises. They have all found a congenial home in the New Deals, Fair Deals, New Frontiers, Great Societies, and New Federalism of our age. Yet, the very environment being created by them affords us something to react against in the same way that our forefathers did, perhaps once again to the benefit of liberty. As the saying goes, good judgment comes from experience, and experience comes from bad judgment.

G. Warren Nutter
The American Revolution

CHAPTER 2

The American political system has often been characterized as a grand social experiment in self-government. The framers of the Constitution constructed a republican system for the express purpose of dispersing, not concentrating, political power and, thereby, economic power. Their motto was, effectively, "the government which governs least, governs best," and they set about establishing a new political order with strict constitutional limitations on the "centres" of governmental decision making and political power. A *federal* republic made up of largely independent states, loosely coordinated by a central administration, was delegated limited responsibilities and powers. At the national level they established a political obstacle course, composed of two houses, a president, and judiciary, through which legislation had to pass before it could become law; they thought few legislative proposals would make their way through this maze.

The founders of this country's social experiment were willing to rely on majority rule not because it was a way of facilitating collective decisions and the control of people by government but because it was a means of restricting the range of issues decided and controlled by politics. In *The Federalist* James Madison defended this governmental organization with unforgettable words:

> *First.* In a single republic, all of the power surrendered by the people is submitted to the administration of a single government; and the usurpations are guarded against by a division of the government into distinct and separate departments. In the compound republic of America, the power surrendered by the people is first divided between two distinct governments, and then the portion allotted to each is subdivided among distinct and separate departments. Hence a

double security arises to the rights of the people. The different governments will control each other, at the same time each will be controlled by itself.

Second. It is of great importance in a republic, not only to guard the society against the oppression of its rulers; but to guard one part of the society against the injustice of the other parts . . . [By way of the federal republic] the society itself will be broken in so many parts, interests, and classes of citizens, *that the rights of individuals, or of the minority, will be in little danger from interested combinations of the majority.* In a free government, the security of civil rights must be the same as that for religious rights. It consists in the one case in the multiplicity of interests, and in the other, in the multiplicity of sects. [Emphasis added.][1]

In short, the framers wanted the power given up by people to government to be dispersed among many different and competing governments—at the federal, state, and local levels. No one level of government would be allowed to have much say over anything. Further, they thought majority rule would restrain government simply because there were few issues on which a majority of the "multiplicity of interests" and "multiplicity of sects" could and would agree. Therefore, few collective decisions usurping the rights of individuals could be expected.

The presuppositions most of the framers took with them to Philadelphia are fairly evident in what they said and did. Rights ultimately spring from individuals, not government. The history of tyranny is the history of the garnering of rights and power by the state. Freedom can be maximized only by the strict containment of the state, by the minimization of the scope and influence of government. The framers were not interested in using government to constrain an otherwise free market; rather, they were interested in fostering the freedom of individuals within the market and political systems as a means of restricting and controlling government.

In the quotation that heads this chapter, the late Warren Nutter, an economist at the University of Virginia, noted the conditions under which the Constitution was devised. At the time, governments in other parts of the world had imposed varied restrictions on people's political and economic freedom. The most casual observer could see the excesses of unchecked governmental power. The framers recognized the necessity of government, but they also recognized the necessity of controlling government. Again, Madison reflects the concern of the time:

> But what is government, but the greatest of all reflections on human nature? If men were angels, no government would be necessary. If angels were to govern men, neither external nor internal controls on government would be necessary. In framing a government, which is to be administered by men over men, the great difficulty lies in this: You must first enable the government to control the governed; and in the next place, oblige it to control itself. A dependence on the people is, no doubt, the primary control on the government; but experience has taught mankind the necessity of auxiliary precautions.[2]

The experience of the past two centuries has, unfortunately, revealed that the framers largely failed to accomplish their goal: to control for their time and future generations the power of government. We have come full circle to the point where individual freedom and individual decision making are gradually being eroded by the encroachment of "governmental freedom" and "collective decision making." Today's government is neither insignificant in terms of resource use nor unimportant in terms of its influence over people's welfare. It has grown and continues to grow. More important, the propensity of people to seek governmental solution of their individual problems seems unbounded. The government is now the "maker" and the "breaker" of economic and political lives. We see all around us the mercantilist controls that, as Warren Nutter notes, were explicitly rejected by the Founding Fathers: "the fixing of prices, wages, and interest rates; the outlawing of forestalling and engrossing; the regulating of the quality of goods; the licensing of labor; the chartering of corporations; and the establishment of state enterprises."[3] Data on growth in government and in its economic influence clearly demonstrate this point.

GOVERNMENTAL GROWTH

FEDERAL OUTLAYS AND EXPENDITURES

Regardless of the measurement used, governmental growth at all levels has been substantial since our country's inception. As revealed in Table 1, the total receipts of the federal government (expressed in

TABLE 1

FEDERAL GOVERNMENT RECEIPTS
1789–1978
(In millions of current dollars)

Year	Receipts
1789–1791	$4.4
1800	$10.8
1850	$43.6
1900	$567.2
1929	$3,862.6
1960	$94,800.0
1970	$194,800.0
1981[a]	$614,400.0
1982[a]	$728,200.0

SOURCES: U.S., Department of Commerce, *Historical Statistics of the United States: Colonial Times to 1970*, (Washington, D.C.: Government Printing Office, 1975); and U.S., Office of the President, *Economic Report of the President, 1980* (Washington, D.C.: Government Printing Office, 1980).

NOTE: [a]Estimate.

current dollars) in 1800 were about $11 million. By 1900 receipts had expanded to $567 million; by 1929, they had grown to almost $4 billion. By 1981 total receipts of the federal government exceeded $600 billion.

These figures are, of course, distorted by the influence of changing prices. One would expect government receipts, and, hence, necessary expenditures to rise with rising prices. However, 100 years after 1800, prices of consumer goods had actually fallen by 50 percent, indicating that the dollars received by the federal government in 1900 could buy more of the country's goods and services—and that government had 52 times more dollars to spend. Prices did not reattain the level of 1800 until about 1929. Granted, both prices and real output quadrupled between 1929 and 1981; however, during that period federal revenues expanded almost 160-fold. Population also increased during the 1929–1980 period; but, even then, on a per capita basis real government receipts rose about 17 times.

The broad sweep of federal government expansion during this century hides recent reductions in the rate of growth of the federal government. Indeed, Roger Freeman, a research fellow at the Hoover Institution, writes in his study of federal government growth:

> Everybody knows that federal spending has been soaring over the past twenty years, far outpacing the growth rate of the nation's economy. Everybody also knows that the federal bureaucracy has dramatically expanded, at a much faster rate than the United States population or the civilian labor force. Everybody, that is, who has not looked at the record.
>
> The fact is—and this may come as a surprise to many usually well-informed persons—that federal expenditures increased in the past twenty years [up until 1972] at about the same rate as the GNP or personal income: they multiplied approximately three and a half times.[4]

Similarly, Thomas Borcherding, economist at Simon Fraser University, found that between 1932 and 1970, total government spending grew at an annual rate of 7 percent. Between 1960 and 1970, on the other hand, government spending grew at a significantly lower rate, 5.1 percent.[5] Furthermore, federal government outlays in 1970 constituted approximately 21 percent of gross national product, one percentage point higher than nine years later.

What, then, is the concern? The principal worry is the shift in the composition of federal government expenditures—what the government now does with its greater purchasing power that it did not once do. Much of the increase was used for welfare purposes—to redistribute the nation's income. Indeed, the 270-fold increase in federal nondefense expenditures between 1929 and 1981 suggests the extent of the decline in the relative importance of defense over the past 50 years. Consequently, the expenditures of the federal government on redistribution now represent a more than 50 percent greater share of the federal budget than they did back in 1929. Before 1900, transfer payments were hardly detectable in the federal budget.

Without question, we have now become a redistributive society. Like it or not, by design or accident, an enormous number of people, perhaps more than 50 percent of the population (no one really knows), obtain a significant part of their income from governmental programs.

Many of these people are truly in need, but most are not. Less than 20 percent of total welfare expenditures is actually intended to help the poor.[6] However, we have with the moneys spent on the poor erected an almost insurmountable "welfare wall" around the poor. For their "welfare" the poor of the country are no longer dependent on work and imagination but on the state. Any income earned by the poor is effectively "taxed" away at phenomenally high marginal rates (reaching up to 80 percent) in the form of reduced welfare benefits.[7] The welfare state has ensured that the poor gain very little from work and investment in job training and education and has, to that extent, seductively entrapped a large number of people in a life of poverty. As George Gilder, author of *Wealth and Poverty*, quipped, "The poor choose leisure [to the extent that they do] not because of moral weakness, but because they are paid to do so."[8] The "double-whammy effect" of transfer payments is also felt by the not-so-poor and high-income earners who must endure the tax wedge caused by transfer payments that separates take-home pay from gross earnings. The "rich" are also induced to choose, on the margin, leisure over work and the assumption of risk that goes with investment. On balance, transfers reduce intragenerational production and redistribute the income earned from the future to the present.

Furthermore, people are concerned about federal government growth because of the growing federal influence over state and local government growth (where expenditures have really been rising) and because of the tendency of the federal government to use its dollars to manage and regulate—that is, to control and, thereby, impose costs on—the private sector. Through regulation, the government also gets more "bang for the buck" because it induces private businesses and citizens to spend their dollars on accomplishing government objectives.

FEDERAL EMPLOYMENT

Federal government employment has risen drastically over the past two centuries. There were just under 5,000 workers on the payroll in 1800. About 240,000 people were employed by the federal government at the turn of the century. By the late 1970s, there were 2.9 million federal workers, about the same number as at the beginning of the decade. Recently, the (apparent) percentage of the labor force working for the federal government decreased substantially, from 3.5 percent in 1959 to 2.8 percent in 1979, as employment in the private sector expanded.

Again, the statistics belie the public's concern over growth in the central government. For several reasons, in spite of the statistics just given, concern over federal government growth is justified. First, the composition of federal employment changed dramatically during 1960s and 1970s. Economists James Bennett and Manuel Johnson of George Mason University point out that blue-collar workers accounted for one-third of the federal labor force in 1959, but for only one-fifth in 1979. The percentage of higher-grade employees of the federal government has grown substantially even though total employment has remained more or less constant.[9] The federal work force has gradually evolved into a managerial class.

Second, total employment figures are not an accurate count of the number of people working directly for the federal government. To minimize the employment count, the federal government has developed a class of workers (probably 20 percent of all federal workers) referred to as "25 and ones." These employees work full-time for 25 of 26 annual pay periods. During the one pay period when the employee count is made, these "25 and ones" are reduced to temporary status and are, therefore, not included in the total employment figures. Such revelations caused Bennett and Johnson to conclude: "The most accurate statement that can be made about employment in the federal sector is that its size is unknown and that any statistics available vastly understate the true number in the total federal work force."[10]

Third, the federal government hires many people indirectly through grants to universities and private research organizations, through consulting contracts, and through quasi-public organizations like the Tennessee Valley Authority. These people are not included in statistics of direct federal employment. Indeed, many federal agencies have little idea just how many people work indirectly for them. The *National Journal* estimated that in 1979 there were at least four indirect federal employees for each person on the federal payroll.[11] These estimates are conservative because the indirect employment of half of the departments could not be estimated. Given the growth in the federal budget, it is fair to suspect that although direct federal employment has decreased in the past few years, *total* federal employment—both direct and indirect—has grown steadily.

STATE AND LOCAL GOVERNMENT

State and local governments have also expanded considerably over past decades. Table 2 shows that in 1902 (the earliest year for which data are available) all state and local governments in the United States had combined receipts of a little more than $1 billion; by 1980 receipts exceeded $382 billion.

TABLE 2

STATE AND LOCAL GOVERNMENT RECEIPTS
1902–1978
(In millions of current dollars)

Year	Receipts
1902	$1,048
1932	$7,887
1960	$25,639
1970	$135,400
1980[a]	$382,600

SOURCES: U.S., Department of Commerce, *Historical Statistics of the United States: Colonial Times to 1970* (Washington, D.C.: Government Printing Office, 1975); and U.S., Office of the President, *Economic Report of the President, 1981* (Washington, D.C.: Government Printing Office, 1981).

NOTE: [a]Preliminary.

Although the federal budget generally rose faster than combined state and local budgets in the early part of this century, the total budgets of state and local governments grew significantly faster than the budget of the federal government during the past two decades. In recent years official employment at the state and local levels has also grown more rapidly than at the federal level. Although employing only 2.5 million people, about 5 percent of the labor force, in 1929, state and local governments hired over 12 million people, approximately 13 percent of the labor force, in 1976. Employment of state and local governments grew especially fast relative to the federal government during the 1970s.

Growth in government can be—and has been—partially explained by the growth in the country's population and income, the increase in "social congestion" (the extent to which we all get in each other's way), the increase in demand for greater quantities and qualities of public goods and services like garbage collection, and the enhanced leadership role that the United States plays in defense of the free world. The irrefutable fact is that government at all levels now accounts for over a third of the country's gross national product and taxes away more than 42 percent of national income. As recently as 1940, the government's role in the economy was far less prominent. Indeed, these statistics obscure the true import of contemporary government. Governments, through exemptions and loopholes in tax codes, induce individuals and businesses to make "socially desirable" expenditures on, for example, charities and business investments that they would otherwise not make. Although these expenditures result from private decisions (manipulated by the tax codes), government accomplishes its purposes as surely as if it had collected taxes and spent the money itself. At the start of this decade these so-called tax expenditures exceeded $269 billion. The government, by regulating individual and business behavior, causes even more of the nation's resources to be diverted from private to public uses. If these forms of government influence could be totaled, which they cannot be with any precision, surely government in the United States would be responsible for directing the use of well over 50 percent of the nation's income.

THE POLITICAL AND ECONOMIC CONSEQUENCES

The trends in governmental economic activity are alarming. This growth in government means that decisions regarding resource use are now made by collective, political institutions. The realm of private decision making—and private responsibility for decisions made—is seriously constricted. As an affront to freedom, this is in itself bad. However, there are other reasons for concern. Many production and distribution decisions are now channeled through the slow, tedious, and inefficient political process. Indeed, we have overburdened the political process with far more decisions than that process can make with any reasonable degree of responsiveness and flexibility. We are using a scarce resource—democracy—as though it were a free good, inexhaustible in supply, and as though the assumption of more responsibility by government has little or no impact on the government's ability to perform its basic functions of providing for defense, law enforcement, and education.

When people make private decisions to engage in private trades, they do so voluntarily—because they choose to do so. Presumably, both parties to a trade gain because of their private decisions. Neither exerts coercion over the other because the gain is mutual. Each party to a potential trade has a private incentive, when decisions are private and voluntary, to seek ways to help the other; that is the only way to achieve the unanimous consent necessary for trades to occur.

Collective, democratic decisions made through government do not, on the other hand, require unanimity. Most of the time democratic decisions require agreement among a simple majority of voters; much of the time, because of reliance on representatives and the committee process and the undue political influence of special interest groups, democratic decisions are made with much less than majority agreement. Indeed, given the reliance on bureaucracy in modern government, many public decisions are made by a handful of unelected government workers.

Growth in government means a movement away from private decisions, which require unanimous agreement but affect relatively few people, to collective decisions, which, although they affect many, can be made by a small group. Growth in government can mean and has meant a growth in the ability of some people—those in agreement and with political clout—to impose their will on others who may or may not be in the minority. John Stuart Mill, in his *Essay on Liberty*, was understandably concerned about the "tyranny of the majority"; former Senator Eugene McCarthy has expressed many of the same sentiments, arguing that government restrictions on political compaigns are "the ultimate tyranny of the majority."[12]

Further, growth in government means a growth in the number of people whose livelihood depends directly on government and its programs. The government has created its own constituency to whom it can turn for the political support it needs for its own growth. Farmers definitely have an interest in the growth of the Department of Agriculture and the subsidies it provides them. University professors would like an expansion of state and federal budgets for education and research. Social security recipients concern themselves with expanded benefits and increased taxes on those who are working and supplying the funds for that system. Workers at Lockheed watch the defense budget. Many, if not most, government employees, of course, have an interest in the growth of virtually all governmental programs: further expansion means an increase in the demand for their services, higher wages, and greater job security.

Governmental expansion can start as a small snowball, with a few people who have a direct interest, and end up as an avalanche of all-encompassing government activity, with a constituency for governmental growth that spans the political spectrum. When government becomes "large," it is very difficult to contract it, to eliminate or significantly reduce programs riddled with waste, inefficiency, and corruption. Each program develops its own constituency that will, when its ox is gored, vocally oppose any cutbacks in the program. Furthermore, a constituency adversely affected by proposed cuts can be expected to use its money in the political arena, buying by campaign contributions and outright bribes the legislative support it needs. We may now be unable to return to a condition of restricted state responsibility. We can only hope not.

Statistics suggest that government in recent decades has grown faster at the local and state levels than it has at the federal level. Some observers have concluded that governmental growth has been accompanied by a relative, if not absolute, dispersion of political power. These statistics, however, hide a general tendency toward greater centralization of power. One of the reasons for the rapid growth of state and local governments is the enormous increase in federal grants, restricted and unrestricted, to state and local governments. In 1902 federal grants represented only 0.7 percent of total state and local revenues. In the late 1970s, federal grants made up about 15 percent of their total revenues. Similarly, federal and state grants to local governments accounted for only 6 percent of local government revenues in 1902. Now, such grants constitute about 35 percent of local government budgets. It follows that much of the growth in state and local government employment is attributable to the growing influence of the federal government. State and local governments have become, to a great extent, arms (or dependent agencies) of the federal government.

The budgetary dependence of local governments on state and federal governments and of state governments on the federal government has increased the political and economic power and the social prominence of the larger governmental units substantially. The growth in dependence has enhanced the leverage of state governments over local governments and of the federal government over both state and local governments. By offering matching grants or by threatening to withdraw previously committed funds, the federal government can entice, induce, and coerce state and local governments to do its bidding, to carry out programs—from highways to hospitals to welfare—that it believes are in the "national interest." In the game of politics, the budgetary dependence of a small government on a larger government spells power and control. The federal government's threat in 1978 to cut off virtually all grants to the University of North Carolina system if it did not mold its employment and admission policies to the dictates of the then Department of Health, Education, and Welfare is a relatively clear example of the arrogance with which governmental power has been and can be exercised.

The economic dependence of state and local governments on higher governmental authority has effectively reduced the independence of and, therefore, competition among governmental units. It has effectively increased the monopoly power of states and the federal government. In a "compound republic," states operate largely independently of one another. In setting tax rates, one state government must consider what other states are doing to their tax rates. Much like a competitor in a private market, each state knows that people and businesses respond to higher prices, or, in the case of states, to higher tax rates. Each state knows that it will lose some of its tax base if it raises its rates above or lowers the quality of services below those prevailing in surrounding states. Although competition among state governments is limited, states still have to compete. The loss of the tax bases of Great Britain and New York City and state, due in part to relatively high tax rates, vividly illustrates what can happen to governments that ignore the limited competition they do face. A state may wish to impose higher tax rates, but competition limits its ability to do that.

Competitors in private markets have an economic incentive to form cartels, like the Organization of Petroleum Exporting Countries (OPEC), that negate market forces and set higher prices for all producers. State governments interested in expansion have a similar incentive to surrender some of their sovereignty to a higher government that, acting like the central administrator of a cartel, subverts competition (by imposing uniform tax rates) among states and raises "tax prices." "What cannot be accomplished by independent, competitive action can be accomplished by collusive, monopoly action" is a rule of economic life just as applicable to competing governments as to competing firms, if not more so. One way state governments can act monopolistically is to allow (or induce) the federal government to collect taxes and pass the revenues back to state governments (or to assume the states' former responsibilities). Usually the states could not have obtained these revenues by independent action. Why else would states go to the trouble of channeling the funds through the inefficient federal bureaucracy? Rather than indicating the dispersion of governmental powers, revenue-sharing funds and federal grants attest to the contemporary concentration and centralization of government.[13] Much of the growth in government conflicts with the goals of the Founding Fathers, and it indicates the extent to which we have become detached from the constitutional framework they established.

GOVERNMENT REGULATION

Government regulation is without question the number-one growth industry in the country. Rules on what we shall wear, how we should work and under what conditions, what we can eat and drink, where we should live and in what kind of houses, and what we can drive flow from the seats of government like lava from an erupting volcano. Because of the growth in regulation, we are now a nation of criminals; no mortal can read, much less comprehend, all of the rules that emanate from the halls of government. As noted in Chapter 1, each person daily violates some rule that he does not know even exists.[14] With considerable naiveté, President Jimmy Carter, during his first year in office, asked his cabinet members to read over the rules of their own departments before imposing them on the public. Most of the secretaries did not even try to follow this directive. Those who tried did nothing else but read; and still they fell behind.

No matter how inconsequential, no social or economic ill seems to escape the attention of social reformers in their missionary quest for perfection in an imperfect world—their zeal to protect us from the perceived perils of daily existence.[15] Social regulation is flagrantly destructive of individual freedom. This concern with the growth in regulation can, within limits, be evaluated in economic terms; in many obvious and not-so-obvious ways, regulation contributes to higher production costs, lower productivity, higher price levels, and lower incomes. The overall impact of government regulation is difficult to assess; the effects are often hidden and obscured in increases in prices and reductions in purchasing power. However, evidence on the destructive effects of regulation continues to mount. Some of the ways regulation affects our economic well-being are briefly outlined below.

The regulation of many industries has distorted the use of the nation's resources, raising production costs and consumer prices. The regulation of natural gas prices, for example, has generated cutbacks in the supply of that product, forcing consumers to alternative, more costly energy sources, such as oil and electricity.[16] Past regulation of natural gas has made us more, not less, dependent on foreign oil suppliers and is, in part, responsible for the growth in the economic power of the Arab countries. Similar regulation of the trucking, airline, communications, banking, insurance, utilities, postal service, legal, and drug industries has had similar distorting, but hidden, economic effects.[17]

Businesses must contend with the flood of regulations that come their way. Just being aware of the applicable regulations imposes considerable costs on businesses. As noted above, describing the economic impact of these regulations is a hazardous task at best. The growth in the page count of the *Federal Register*, which records all rules, regulations, and notices issued daily by federal agencies, is one, albeit limited and imperfect, means of illustrating the problems businesses face in just keeping up. As Figure 1 reveals, the *Federal Register* had only 2,411 pages back in 1936, a mere two volumes. By 1950, only 4,910 pages had been added to the *Register*. By the end of 1980, however, the *Federal Register*, containing more words per page, was adding pages at an annual rate of 87,011, 44 percent higher than the number of total pages in 1975. Between 1970 and 1980, the *Register* grew at an annual compound rate of nearly 16 percent.

Granted, the *Federal Register* contains much material unrelated to what businesses can and cannot do. On the other hand, single sentences can contain requirements that can cause businesses to spend millions, if not billions, of dollars. Rules inspired by the politics of Washington can significantly reduce the flexibility of the economy to respond to changing conditions. Rights given to one group, for example, workers, may no longer be rights that can be traded. When the Occupational Safety and Health Administration mandates certain safety regulations, firms

Figure 1

Growth in the Federal Register

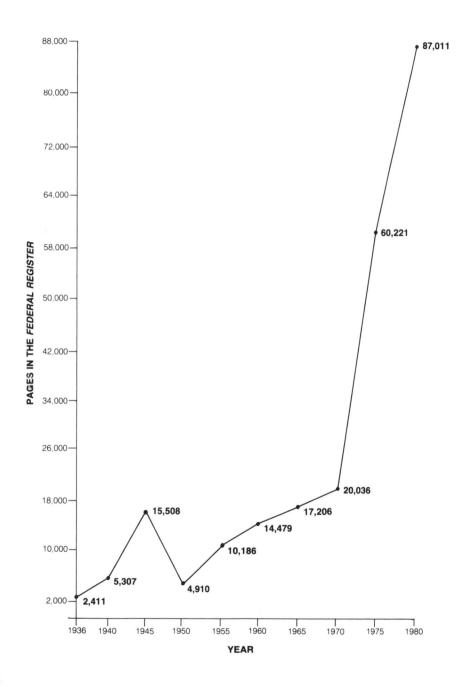

lose the right to pay workers to take the risk associated with slightly more hazardous working conditions and workers lose the right to accept higher pay for assuming more hazardous conditions of work. Furthermore, regulations have a tendency to become fixed, unchangeable even when considerable evidence of their ineffectiveness or destructiveness is amassed.

Regulations increase the budgets of governments and the tax demands placed on citizens and are a significant cause of governmental growth. Table 3 reveals the budgetary cost of federal regulations between 1970 and 1977. During that period the budgets of economic and social regulatory agencies grew fivefold, expanding by over 26 percent per year.

The regulatory activity of governments imposes substantial compliance costs on businesses. Economists Murray Weidenbaum and Robert Defina conservatively estimated the annual compliance cost in 1976 at nearly $63 billion (about 4 percent of that year's gross national product).[18] *Less* conservative estimates put the annual compliance cost at over $130 billion in 1977; surely, the figure is much larger today, considering inflation and the greater number of regulations.

A considerable portion of the compliance costs of government regulations is reflected in the time that business people spend filling out government forms. James Bennett and Manuel Johnson estimate that in 1977 the federal government alone had a total of 5,473 *repetitive* forms for businesses to complete. These forms required 427 million responses, and businesses conservatively spend an estimated 210 million man-hours on federal paperwork, a 36 percent increase over 1973. These figures do not include the more than 600 million man-hours people and businesses spend each year filling out their tax returns and the millions of man-hours businesses spend each year filling out non-repetitive forms.[19] Bennett and Johnson figure that in 1980 the paperwork burden for individuals and businesses easily exceeded a billion (and very likely approached two billion) man-hours.[20] And, it should be noted, a billion man-hours represents a "disguised" federal work force of 500,000 full-time employees.

Someone must deal with the regulatory agencies, and often the workload falls on the shoulders of top executives. Peter Drucker, professor of social sciences at Claremont Graduate School, estimates that over 60 percent of the time of top management in large- and medium-sized companies is spent on outside relations: "Traditionally

American top managements have given about three-fourths of their time to managing the day-to-day business. Most still try today—but they have only a fifth of their time available for the job."[21] Certainly, the efficiency of any company must suffer when the boss is away so much. Clearly, there now exists a whole cadre of company officers who do nothing but deal with "government (as distinct from public) relations" and who now have a vested interest in the continued regulation of the private sector, the area of their expertise.

Finally, regulations affect the productivity of the American worker. Because resources are diverted into the regulatory process, more resources must be used to maintain any given level of output. Regulations tend to reduce business productivity. The ongoing flow of regulations coming from government has eaten into the growth in business productivity. Edward Denison, a senior fellow at the Brookings Institution, estimates that regulations in the two areas of environment and worker health and safety alone had by 1975 reduced the long-term growth in business productivity by 17 percent or more.[22] The growth in regulations very likely was a major reason behind the inconsequential rise in U.S. productivity in late 1970s.

Regulations that affect the rate of growth in productivity also affect the rate of inflation. The basic cause of persistent inflation can be stated very simply: the rate of growth in the money stock exceeds the rate of growth of goods and services. A 12 percent rate of growth in the money stock, when output expands by 2 percent, leads to a 10 percent rate of inflation. Regulations have effectively reduced the rate of growth in output, causing any growth in the money stock to have a greater effect on prices.

CONSUMER PROTECTION

Consumerism, which is a special category of business and social regulation, has spurred much governmental growth. It is, moreover, promoted by people who seem to have little philosophic appreciation or analytic comprehension of the role of the individual in the operation of a free society. The assumption is widely made, confidently even if generally implicitly, that government regulation of consumer products not only *can* but surely *will* enhance consumer welfare.

Table 3

Indexes of Growth in Federal Regulation
1970–1977

| Year | Number of Major Regulatory Agencies | | Expenditures of Major Regulatory Agencies (in millions of dollars) | | |
	Economic[a]	Social[b]	Economic[c]	Social[d]	Total
1970	8	12	166.1	1,449.3	1,615.4
1971	8	14	196.8	1,882.2	2,079.0
1972	8	14	246.3	2,247.5	2,493.8
1973	8	17	198.7	2,773.7	2,972.4
1974	9	17	304.3	3,860.1	4,164.4
1975	10	17	427.6	4,251.4	4,679.0
1976	10	17	489.8	5,028.3	5,518.1
1977	10	17	917.1[e]	7,318.3[e]	8,235.4[e]
Percentage increase (1970–1977)	25	42	452	405	410
Compounded percentage increase per year			27.6	26.0	26.2

SOURCES: For 1970–1975, see William Lilley III and James C. Miller III, "The New Social Regulation," *Public Interest*, Spring 1977, p. 50; for 1976–1977, update provided by Keith McGowan, in James C. Miller and Bruce Yandle, eds., *Benefit-Cost Analysis of Social Regulations: Case Studies from the Council on Wage and Price Stability* (Washington, D.C.: American Enterprise Institute, 1979), pp. 2–3.

NOTES: [a] Agencies included: Civil Aeronautics Board, Commodity Futures Trading Commission (1975–1977), Federal Communications Commission, Federal Energy Administration (1974–1977), Federal Maritime Commission, Federal Power Commission, Federal Trade Commission, International Trade Commission (1974–1977), Interstate Commerce Commission, Securities and Exchange Commission, and Tariff Commission (1970–1973).

[b] Agencies included: Agricultural Marketing Service (1972–1977), Atomic Energy Commission (1970–1974), Consumer and Marketing Service (1970–1971), Coast Guard, Consumer Product Safety Commission (1973–1977), Employment Standards Administration (1971–1977), Environmental Protection Agency, Equal Employment Opportunity Commission, Federal Aviation Administration, Federal Highway Administration, Federal Railroad Administration, Food and Drug Administration, Mining Enforcement and Safety Administration (1973–1977), National Highway Traffic Safety Administration, National Labor Relations Board, National Transportation Safety Board (1971–1977), Nuclear Regulatory Commission (1975–1977), Occupational Safety and Health Administration (1973–1977), Occupational Safety and Health Review Commission (1971–1977), ard Workplace Standards Administration.

[c] Taken from the Budget of the United States, 1972–1977.

[d] Taken from the Budget of the United States, 1972–1977. Total includes all expenditures of the agencies listed in note b above except health- and safety-related expenditures for the following agencies: Atomic Energy Commission (1970–1974: "regulatory activities"), Coast Guard ("operating expenses": merchant marine safety, marine law enforcement, marine environmental protection), Federal Aviation Administration ("operations": flight standards program, medical standards program; "facilities": engineering and development; and "safety regulation"), Federal Highway Administration ("motor carrier and highway safety"), and Federal Railroad Administration ("Bureau of Railroad Safety").

[e] Estimated.

Consumer advocates would have us believe that society is some sort of "anthropomorphic whole," with a mind, a will, and a preference of its own independent of the people who make up society and that they, the consumer advocates, have the expertise needed to decide what society wants or should have. In many ways, the consumer movement epitomizes the intellectual attitude that pervades much modern discussion of social reform and motivates the expansion of much government activity.

Instead of passively accepting the claims of consumer protectionists, consumers—that is, everyone—should consider past government efforts to protect consumers. Historical experience suggests that putting government in charge of protecting the consumer forces us to address another question that is often overlooked: "How do we regulate the regulators?" "How do we protect consumers from the protectors?" Several concrete examples can explain why these questions are central to the debate over consumer protection.

THE COST OF PROTECTION

All of us are interested in product quality, product safety, and getting what we bargain for. Opposition to such things borders on insanity. It is like being against motherhood or apple pie. Everyone would like to be able to buy goods, from appliances to meat to automobiles, that are perfectly or nearly safe, and everyone would like to leave a store perfectly confident that he or she got full value for the money. No one likes buying hamburger, for instance, and finding out later that the meat in the center of the package is several days old.

The point here is that product quality and safety and consumer confidence, far from being undesirable, are desired by almost everyone. However, product quality and safety and consumer confidence in the product come, more often than not, at a cost—often at a very high cost. No one would object to greater safety and higher quality if they are free or demand no sacrifice. On the other hand, consumer advocates, if they are sincerely concerned about consumer welfare, should remember that the overworked adage "You can't have your cake and eat it too" contains a simple truth.

In reality, many of the things proposed by consumer advocates are goods in themselves. They carry a price and will continue to do so whether the economy is privately or governmentally run. Granted the government can subsidize safety improvements or regulate production, but this spells higher taxes. There is only one major difference between paying for something through a price increase and paying for it through a tax increase. Under the tax system, someone other than the consumer who benefits from the purchase can be forced to make the payment.

Once we have recognized the potential cost of increased product safety or enhanced quality, the problem of whether a product should be made safer or its quality enhanced is no longer simple. This is because not all consumers demand the same amount of safety, given the price, just as not all consumers demand the same number of record albums by Kiss or the Sex Pistols, given the prices of those albums. Society is not the anthropomorphic whole speaking with one voice that consumer advocates would have us believe. *Diversity*, not uniformity, is the hallmark of society, and the economic system that serves society must reflect this.

Indeed, presuming that individuals need and will choose to buy, regardless of price, a given level of safety is a grossly simplistic and paternalistic view of human behavior. Consumers are often willing to forgo safety, because of the cost, in deference to other things. Some are even willing to forgo health and years of life in order to have other things now. People smoke even though they know that smoking is harmful. Poor people buy cheap, less-than-reliable electric appliances because by doing so, they can have more of other things.

The technology for reducing the number of plane crashes in this country is available. All we have to do is to treat every plane as though it were Air Force One. But, if we did, how many would be willing to pay the price to fly from their hometown to Chicago?

True, in a world in which government is unrestrained by strict constitutional restrictions, Congress can legislate anything the majority or even a minority wishes. The government can require safer cars; it can make even greater efforts to ensure that every can of beans, that every electric appliance, is completely harmless. But what are the costs of doing these things? What must be given up? Will the improvements, if any, be sufficient to warrant the attendant sacrifices? Who will decide whether a product is worth the attendant sacrifices?

Researchers in the Food and Drug Administration (FDA), for example, may know the relationship between an individual's caloric and vitamin intake and his health and lifespan; they may know that headrests reduce the severity of injuries in automobile accidents; and they may know in how many seconds a given material can be consumed by flames. However, there is one thing they do not know—other people's preferences, including their willingness to assume risk. To that extent, so-called experts are poor judges of what anyone else should buy.

This is not an indictment of all government intervention in the market. For example, the case for requiring producers to provide consumers with reasonably full and accurate information about products is strong. The cost of informative labeling, including ingredients and nutritional breakdown, is trivial. Within bounds, such labeling can greatly reduce the costs consumers bear in gathering information and still leave the individual the choice of what to buy. There is, however, a vast difference between requiring information disclosures and making a given product meet certain standards. The former enlightens choice; the latter eliminates it. Furthermore, there are strict limits on how much information disclosure can be mandated before the space on a bottle is used up or the consumer is overwhelmed with more information than he can comprehend or use.[23]

WHOSE PUBLIC INTEREST?

The imposition of controls and standards appears to be a rather easy, direct solution to complex problems. All we need do, so the argument goes, is establish regulations in the *public interest*, set up a regulatory body, and hand over to its members the power to regulate in the public interest. Although controls may be desirable in some cases, this popular impression of them is deceptively naive. For one thing, people disagree. Many car buyers disagree violently with Ralph Nader over whether the VW beetle should be allowed on the road. Some sports enthusiasts disagree with Mr. Nader on whether they should be allowed to choose to eat at ball games the hot dogs and beer that Mr. Nader declares to be "unhealthful." In short, much of the time the public interest is unclear. Where there is disagreement, rules and regulations reflect the wishes of one faction at the expense of another. The regulations will nonetheless be made by members of a regulatory agency who have their own preferences, biases, and prejudices and who may have no firmer grasp of the public's interest than does anyone else.

CONSUMER PROTECTION IN THE PAST

The social desirability of expanded consumer protection can be assessed largely in terms of the use that government has made of its historical regulatory powers. We must mistrust many consumer proposals not because government is inherently evil but because much technical research and everyday experience has shown that in the name of consumer protection the consumer has been exploited by special interest groups seeking to improve their own economic position behind the veil of government regulation. The following examples are culled from a long and disheartening list of cases.

● We have legislated that every car buyer purchase two headrests and six sets of seat belts—but how many people use them? Twenty-five percent of the driving public? Do idle seat belts do anyone any good, aside from the producers who support the rules and those who insist that everyone buy them?

● In the fall of 1977, Secretary of Transportation Brock Adams came out in support of mandatory installation of air bags in new automobiles. Although these devices could be obtained on a special order basis, most people have chosen not to buy them—that is, at the price they would have to pay. Proponents of air bags are apparently oblivious to the social consequences of the forced use of such safety devices. We know from unhappy experience that the number of accidents and deaths on highways is highly correlated to reckless driving. We know also that the amount of reckless driving is related to the cost that drivers bear in the event of an accident. Since air bags reduce some costs of personal injury to the driver, we can expect that mandatory air bags will lead to increased reckless driving and to increased accident rates. And, in fact, many automobile safety regulations have had this perverse effect: they have increased the number of accidents.[24]

● There are seemingly plausible theoretical arguments in support of requiring inspections of automobile headlights, brakes, and other equipment. However, according to economist Mark Crain of Virginia Tech, such regulations have had no detectable effect on the level of automobile accidents. The regulations have, however, handed over to service stations and garages a measure of monopoly power to force consumers to have more extensive, even if doubtfully effective, inspections and repairs than they would otherwise choose.[25]

• Proposals for reinstituting price controls, similar to the ones in effect during the Nixon administration, are repeatedly heard. The proposals are, of course, advocated in the name of consumer protection. But such controls are always ineffective—and for good reason: the task of efficiently controlling the price of virtually everything is simply too complex for any government.[26] And, ironically, the prices of those things that government has controlled directly or indirectly—including utilities, insurance rates, taxicab fares, plane and train ticket prices, and postal rates—have ranked high on the list of price increases over the years.[27] With that record and with the steady rise in taxes, we must wonder again who needs protection from whom.

• When an industry's sales are particularly depressed, imports are usually blamed. This was the case in 1977 when the Carter administration imposed a tariff on imported televisions as one of its first domestic economic acts. The expressed concern was that the Japanese were taking over the U.S. television market (with better and cheaper products, I might add). Now, because of the tariff, we pay higher prices for Sony TV's. Increasing the cost of consumer purchases by a governmentally imposed tariff is commonplace. Indeed, the tariff code of the United States is thicker than the Los Angeles telephone directory. When tariffs are imposed, who is being protected? The consumer? Hardly. Every tariff is backed by a special interest to the detriment of the general public's interest. This occurs because the interest of consumers is politically diffused and, therefore, politically latent, while the interest of those who seek protection is politically concentrated and, therefore, politically kinetic. As economists have stressed for centuries, most justifications devised by producers for tariffs form a smoke screen hiding the natural desire of businesses to avoid competition. When tariffs are common, businessmen sense the correctness of that position. They may gain from the protection they individually receive, but they lose from the protection afforded all other industries. They, too, are consumers who must pay higher prices for everything they buy.

• In the past Congress legislated that banks could not pay interest on checking accounts. In times of tight money banks tried to attract deposits by giving away anything from pots and pans to trading stamps and shotguns. One bank even "sold" money at a 20 percent discount. There is nothing reprehensible about trying to attract deposits, but these were inefficient means of paying interest. Fortunately, in the early 1980s government moved to decontrol (in a limited way) interest rates on all bank accounts.

• Largely to protect the poor, there are limitations on what lenders can charge. But experience has taught the most certain way to ensure that the poor are unable to obtain consumer credit is to control the interest rate on consumer loans. High interest rates may be lamentable but the poor reveal by their borrowing that they prefer loans at high (market-clearing) rates to no credit at low (shortage-inducing) rates.

• We have tried to legislate high medical standards, and we have many superbly trained doctors. But we also have people who, because of monopolistic high prices, go without professional medical care or turn to quacks or home remedies that may be unsafe, ineffective, or inappropriate.[28]

• Every state in the union has a plethora of government-enforced cartelized rules and regulations governing entrance into various trades, like barbering, and professions, like law. The regulations were proffered as ways of protecting consumers from "unethical" and "unqualified" operators. The effect has been to restrict the supply of workers in the regulated areas and to increase the prices consumers pay.[29] Further, as some consumers have learned, state licenses do little to distinguish the competent from the incompetent operators. After bearing the costs of restricted competition, they still must search out the quality of service they want.

• Since 1962, we have required drug manufacturers to prove to the satisfaction of the FDA that new drugs are safe and effective. The purpose has been to save lives, to avoid the tragic Thalidomide problem. However, the new regulation has increased the gestation period for new drugs from two to as much as eight years. The average period is four years, twice what it was before 1962.[30]

The new law has probably saved lives that would have been lost by the introduction of unsafe drugs, but it has resulted also in the loss of lives that would have been saved if certain new drugs had been available sooner. For example, a drug used in mental health therapy that was not introduced in the United States until 1971 was available in Europe five years earlier. The five-year delay may have resulted in 1,200 preventable deaths.[31]

Over the past several years, studies have found that FDA safety and efficacy requirements result in more deaths than lives saved. Furthermore, these requirements reduce competition among drug manufacturers and increase medication bills.[32] Sam Pelztman, an economist at the University of Chicago, who has studied drug regulations extensively, concludes:

> In a wider perspective, any attempt to minimize the risk in the area [of drug development] has costs which (according to the history of drug development) far exceed the benefits: Those who will suffer death and disease while a potential drug therapy is evaluated will suffer no less than the victims of a drug disaster, but their number is likely to be much larger than the number of victims of the disaster . . . The unequal emphasis placed on the benefits and costs of risk taking may be explained, if not excused, by the contrast beween the anonymity of the beneficiaries and the visibility of the victims.[33]

● In 1976, the FDA ruled that producers of cold, cough, allergy, and antihistamine products could no longer claim that their products "loosen congestion so you can cough it up or get it off your chest" or "promote free breathing" or "free secretions along the lower respiratory tract." Instead, manufacturers could claim only that, for example, their product increases "expectorant action to loosen phlegm (sputum) and bronchial secretion" and "relieves irritated membranes in the respiratory passageway by preventing dryness through increased mucous flow."[34] Do even the more sophisticated among us have, because of the new labels, any better idea of what these products do?

In 1975, the Federal Trade Commission (FTC) proposed a similar rule for advertising of over-the-counter cold and allergy products. Fortunately, that rule was rejected early in 1981. However, the bureaucratic contest that was waged reveals the true waste of much proposed regulation. The debate took five years and drained nearly 20,000 man-hours from the staff of the FTC. It also led to 4,230 pages of transcript of hearings, 2,300 pages of documents submitted by the FTC, and 6,000 pages of exhibits and rebuttal comments by outsiders; and it cost the federal government an additional $61,000. The informal hearings, by themselves, involved fifty expert witnesses. The administrative and legal fees incurred by one trade association to fight the rule totaled more than $2 million; other trade associations spent smaller amounts. As Clemson University economist Bruce Yandle muses in an article on the FTC proceedings, the whole expensive process is troublesome because the FTC was simply following the procedures outlined in the Magnuson-Moss Act of 1975, which requires the FTC to conduct oral hearings, allow for cross-examinations, and provide for rebuttals—and this process must be followed every step of the way, no matter how inane the proposed rules may be. (A similar set of procedures was, at the time of this writing, being considered for every major deregulation effort, no matter how unreasonable, ineffective, or inefficient the regulation is believed to be.) Yandle suggests that the advertisers may have only won a temporary truce, not a victory. With a change in commissioners or political climate, the FTC staff could give notice of another set of rules, giving rise to more years of expensive hearings.[35]

• In a recent study funded by the Department of Housing and Urban Development, researchers found that "excessive government regulations" were responsible for some $10,000 of the cost of a three-bedroom, $50,000 house.[36] Congress's occasional flirtation with establishing a consumer protection agency whose principal task would be to protect the consumer from the other protective agencies in Washington is understandable.

• In 1965, the owner of a midwestern trucking firm, who found that the railroads invariably protested any proposed rate reduction he submitted to the Interstate Commerce Commission (ICC), offered to transport yak fat from Omaha to Chicago for 45 cents per hundred pounds.[37] As expected, the railroads protested to the ICC: the new rates were obviously predatory. The ICC suspended the yak fat rates and formed committees to study the yak fat rate structure. Only after serious deliberation did the ICC discover that yak fat had not only never been produced in the country, it had never even been sold in the country. One may suspect that the regulators do not always know what they are doing.

Indeed, the evidence suggests that we should question the actual purpose of regulatory bodies like the ICC, which give the impression that they have the interest of consumers at heart. George Stigler, after years of investigating the record of regulatory agencies that control the prices of specific industries, concluded that for a long time we have deluded ourselves into believing regulation is thrust on industries by Congress and state legislatures, whereas it may be more accurate to say that industries deliberately procure regulation in the interest of reducing competition, dividing the market, and setting prices.[38] Again, how do we regulate the regulators?

• In 1977, Secretary of Agriculture Bob Bergland proposed that the government raise the price-support level of milk. The net effect was that consumers paid more for milk.[39] In support of the proposal, Secretary Bergland contended that the costs farmers face had risen and, as a result, there was less milk available on grocery store shelves. To counter this prospect, he argued that we needed to raise the price of milk even higher than it would otherwise have been. This could be expected to increase the amount of milk supplied; we could with equal confidence have expected people to reduce the amount demanded. The resulting surplus meant increased government inventories of unused dairy products and, probably, some milk destroyed. The cost of this scheme to consumers and taxpayers had already exceeded $1.5 billion a year by 1980.

• The government has stipulated that children's sleepwear must be fire resistant. Given the controversy that Trist caused, it would seem that the government did not know what it was getting into when it mandated the order. But it richly deserves the inconvenience. Should not the consumer be able to ask: "If I am willing to take the precaution of keeping matches from my children and to pay for smoke alarms and a house that has a low probability of catching fire, why can I not have my children sleep in plain, simple cotton unadulterated with all those chemicals?"

Why not individual choice? Whatever happened to *individual* discretion, judgment, and responsibility? Unfortunately, the series of examples presented here is not unrepresentative of the effects government regulations have. They are only the tip of a huge iceberg of ill-conceived and misguided regulatory efforts.

THE POLITICIZED SOCIETY

As is obvious from the contents of this chapter, I am concerned about governmental growth and what it portends for the future of the American economy and way of life. I am concerned because I know that government expenditures and regulations did not "just happen" or fall like manna from heaven; they emerged from the political process. Many programs arose because of the actions of people who, although altruistic, were, to repeat William Simon's phrase, "intellectual basket cases" when it came to understanding the market system and government efforts to control that system.[40] However, we cannot, I believe, hang all of our troubles on the social zealots in our midst. We must recognize that many government programs and much regulation faced by business were business-inspired. Many programs and much regulation were conceived not to achieve some noble social purpose but to promote the private interests of some business or industry group. Much of the observed growth in government reflects the use of government by many other special interest groups, with and without business connections, for their own ends, as business did in the past.

The current size and growth of government should be alarming to Americans of all backgrounds, rich and poor, for several reasons. Political maneuvering has become an accepted way of life. After years of attempting to erect the Great Society through government, we have constructed instead the Politicized Society. Indeed, it is taken for granted these days that any group with political influence not only will but *should* use that influence. Far too many people approach the government with their hands cupped in front of them; far too many people take the attitude that if they do not accept government handouts in the guise of economic support and control of markets, someone else will and the world will be no better for their individual restraint. Far too many people shirk responsibility for their own actions and for the welfare of others with the all too easily chanted refrains "Let the government do it" and "There oughta be a law."

The prominence of government in modern society has contributed in subtle ways to the breakdown of the basic principle of honesty, without which any social fabric will come unraveled. Many people who are honest with friends and family think nothing of cheating the government, either claiming more benefits from government programs than they deserve or paying less in taxes than the law requires. Examples of individuals' cheating the government abound: the university professor released from one job in the spring who accepts an offer from another college for the fall but does not sign the contract in order to qualify for unemployment compensation during the summer months; the professional society that organizes a meeting in a foreign country in order to allow members to count vacation expenses as tax deductions; and the government employee who fraudulently secures welfare payments from the programs his agency administers. Each cheater can reason that his individual actions have virtually no effect on government programs and the taxes imposed on others. One person simply does not count in the context of a large government budget. In addition, friends of cheaters are unlikely to object to (and may even support) the actions of those who cheat; they know that this cheating does not significantly affect their own welfare. In short, a level of cheating unacceptable in private relationships is quite rational when government is large and impersonal.

Each year Congress passes about a thousand new laws; state and local governments add thousands more. The executive branch of the federal government now produces more than ten thousand "administrative laws" annually.[41] As government encroaches on new areas of social interaction, the judicial system must produce by rendering decisions thousands of "judicial laws" designed to fill the gaps in laws produced by legislatures and government bureaucracies. The growth in government seriously threatens the stability and durability of the legal system in this country. Our legal system is grounded on the principle that "ignorance of the law is no defense." With the onslaught of new laws, however, judges cannot expect people to abide by that principle; ignorance of the law must at some point become, albeit in limited ways, an acceptable defense. Acceptance of ignorance as a defense could undermine the legal system by absolving people of a basic social responsibility and make justice an uncertain, precarious event. Government officials cannot possibly enforce all the many laws on the books. Enforcement must be selective, partially dependent upon the whim, prejudices, political aspirations, and immediate circumstances of the enforcers. When laws abound, justice becomes suspect and loses much of its moral force. Again, we can no longer afford to treat government as a free good—as if it can do everything in a costless manner.

As George Stigler has warned, "The state—the machinery and power of the state—is a potential resource or threat to every industry in the society. With its power to prohibit or compel, to take or give money, the state can and does selectively help or hurt a vast number of industries."[42] With the considerable power the state presently has to protect firms from competition, to redistribute income from one sector of society (not necessarily the rich) to another (not necessarily the poor), and, in general, to determine the absolute and relative well-being of almost everyone, we should not be surprised that all special interest groups—businesses, consumers, workers, welfare recipients—have begun to direct their energies away from the market toward the political arena and a competitive struggle for political favors.

Firms are interested in making a profit. In private markets the competitive struggle for profits leads them to produce what consumers want and to restrict long-run profits. When government is small with little power to redistribute income or to determine people's welfare, businesses have little incentive to invest resources in lobbying, bribing, or in other ways trying to manipulate government. There is simply little that government can do to help them in securing profits. However, when government is large and has considerable power, as it does today, firms view huge public budgets as a source of profits. Their resources can be used in two ways: investment in capital goods that can be used to produce a product for sale in competitive markets, or investment in lobbying and bribing politicians and in trying to develop legislation that will protect firms from competition or provide them with a share of the public budget. Under a large government, "political investment" can become relatively more profitable than "market investment," and a shift in investment from the market to the political arena should be expected. In private competitive markets, a firm must appeal to buyers to enter mutually beneficial trades; in political markets it can enlist the power of the state to force people to give up part of their income for the firm's benefit.[43]

Businesses can also reason that if they do not enlist the power of the state in an effort to secure an income, then other firms and groups will. Those who refrain may be forced to pay for the political favors secured by others. Sadly, all groups—environmentalists, educators, union members, government employees, electricians, pacifists, farmers, students, welfare recipients, and consumers—can, when government is powerful, follow business groups into the political arena, a trend that threatens to destroy the democratic system by the sheer burden of political conflict and turn the productive society into the politicized society.

In government, "small is beautiful." The great need of today is for people to recognize that simple fact and to understand that the case for the free market is constructed largely on the premise that people should not be free to use the power of the state to protect themselves from the forces of competition in free exchanges between individuals.

Many people misinterpret the case for the free market as a case for free, unbridled human passions and power. They worry that in a world unfettered by government programs and controls, markets will be controlled by unprincipled, greedy, profit-maximizing, capitalist pigs. These people fail to understand that moving from reliance on the market to reliance on the government does not necessarily uplift the integrity of the unscrupulous among us and does not secure the "pursuit of happiness." Rather, the shift from markets to government gives the unscrupulous a new resource—the coercive power of government—through which all of the supposed evils of the market can and will be magnified. The following chapters argue that the case for the free market is built on restricting power by dispersing it among free individuals. The message is urgent and difficult to convey. Fortunately, as Warren Nutter reminds us, at least now government has shown its hand and we have something to react against.

The
Primacy
of the
Individual

If we knew how freedom would be used, the case for it would largely disappear.

Friedrich Hayek
The Constitution of Liberty

CHAPTER 3

U nder overcast skies on a battlefield in Pennsylvania,
President Lincoln read from the back of an envelope: "Four
score and seven years ago our fathers brought forth on this
continent, a new nation, conceived in Liberty, and dedicated to the
proposition that all men are created equal." Those words, drawn from
the heart, have echoed through generations, reminding us of the ultimate price freedom often commands. Lincoln spoke of the equality of
men, but nowhere on that day must the *inequality* of men have been
more apparent than at Gettysburg. Some men lay dead and buried
virtually beneath Lincoln's feet while others stood in the rain and
listened. Equality? Hardly.

If God meant to create men equal in fact, then he botched the job.
Instead of sameness unifying us in one homogeneous mass, differences
separate us all and define our individuality. Skin color is the most
pronounced trait and has been the most troublesome division. However, we also differ dramatically in size, shape, talent, temperament,
circumstance, intelligence, adaptability, productivity, tastes, expecta-
tions, agility, beauty, refinement, and background. We are all human,
but such a statement only defines the broad boundaries of differences.
Categories of differences, which language requires us to use, only hide
the infinite variety.

Any social system designed to serve the ends of all, as opposed to
the ends of a few, must consider the great, readily observable diversity
of humanity. Surprisingly, the case for freedom in general and free
markets in particular is grounded on a relatively simple and innocuous
observation: We are not the same. If we were cut from the same mold,

then the preferences and abilities of any one person would be fully duplicated in everyone else. Life would, I suspect, be utterly dull. More important, there would be no need for a social system that took advantage of our *relative* advantages in production, which are the consequence of differences in our abilities; there would be no need for a social system that ferreted out what each of us wants because each person could readily and accurately reflect what everyone else wants. The tremendous complexity in social relationships due to present differences would not exist; the world would not be uncomplicated; but it would, comparatively speaking, be simple. The case against dictatorial rule would be greatly weakened. The uses to which freedom would be put could be predicted with approximately the same accuracy by any person. As Nobel laureate Friedrich Hayek reminds us in the quotation heading this chapter, the case for freedom in such a world would largely evaporate.

This chapter, while about the "individual," is also about freedom. As this and the following chapters show, freedom requires that the moral significance of the individual be asserted and that, under law, each of us must count for one. Although unequal, we must be treated as equals under the rule of law. There is a subtle but important distinction between *being* equal and *being treated* as equals. This distinction, and what it implies about the role of government in society, has apparently eluded many critics of the free market system. It is, however, a distinction that Lincoln must have had in mind that memorable day on the Gettysburg Battlefield.

THE MORAL SIGNIFICANCE OF THE INDIVIDUAL

The building block of a free society must be the individual, not as a personality, but as an entity respected for its own sake. The individual must have rights to move and shape, within limits, his world. As John Stuart Mill, the nineteenth-century political economist, noted: "The only freedom which deserves the name, is that of pursuing our own good in our own way." Freedom implies the power to imagine a "less unsatisfactory" world, to use a phrase of Ludwig von Mises, and to change the present state of things. Freedom implies purposeful action grounded in power, albeit limited power.

If all actions were fixed by God (as some theologians suggest) or were the product of the myriad forces in our social and physical environment (as some modern sociologists contend), there would be no room for purposeful action because all actions would be predetermined. An individual would possess no power because each person would be fully controlled by forces not under his control; no original or reflective thought would have any real world meaning; there would be no meaning to existence except existence—there would be no concept of freedom.

The psychologist B. F. Skinner, who has spent his professional career attempting to convince his students and the general public that our acts reflect our genetic makeup, our environment, and our personal history, gives us a pretty accurate description of the role of freedom in a deterministic world: "The hypothesis that man is not free is essential to the application of scientific method to the study of human behavior. The free man who is held responsible for the behavior of the external biological organism is only a prescientific substitute for the kinds of causes which are discovered in the course of a scientific analysis."[1] In an important attack on Skinnerism, Tibor Machan, a philosopher, writes:

> Skinner derives his idea of man as a bundle of behavior, an organism moving about, that has no mind, no capacity for initiating action, no freedom, and certainly no dignity. If man is not divine—and if he is a part of nature then that is impossible—he must be a machine. This is the road from Descartes, a supernaturalist from the 16th century, to Skinner, superempiricist and radical behavioralist of the 20th century. Absolutely no contribution of the science of psychology was required to accomplish the transition.[2]

We could search a long time for foolproof arguments and spend many pages trying to rebut Skinner's position that people are incapable of even the smallest degree of freedom, but we would do so in vain. "That men are capable of freedom" is one of those premises that can be asserted but never proven. However, it is a starting point for any meaningful discussion of the organization of human society. If human behavior consists only of responses to external stimuli as opposed to purposeful actions of thinking, original people, there is no need to talk about principles of human organization. That which will exist, exists. We could conceivably talk about the evolution of human events, but there could be no meaningful discussion about improvements—purposeful changes in the course of events. All talk about social institutions, if it arose at all, would itself be a meaningless response to external stimuli, to genetics, and to the evolving social and physical world in which we live. In evaluating this view of the world, one can only wonder why people like Skinner are concerned with the educational environment, with the drug problem, or with mental disorders.

Without freedom, behavior has no moral content, It is neither ethical nor unethical, good nor bad, right nor wrong. Behavior is simply behavior. If given freedom, men can make a hell on earth for themselves and for others. But, as so many social philosophers have pointed out, men must have the freedom to create hell in order to have any meaningful opportunity to strive for heaven, that is, to behave morally.

Freedom must, therefore, be construed as a principle of social organization valuable in itself, distinguishable from its use in any particular circumstance. Freedom must be judged by how it is used on balance over a sequence of individual and social events through time. Freedom is a long-term social contract that people must have with one another. People must have freedom to do things that may be considered repugnant by many in order that they may also have the freedom to do things that meet with approbation. If a person is denied the right to attend any plays but those of Shakespeare, freedom hardly exists except for those who impose their preferences on others. We could conclude that many people are brainless when it comes to making choices and that they should be denied the freedom to make choices. But that means that we transfer power from many individuals to the few individuals deemed capable of making good choices. To whom do we entrust that power? How can we be certain that the power will not be handed over to bad people? Who will tell us what good and bad choices are? Do we hand over to religious leaders the power to make our religious choices? Which ones? The Ayatollah Khomeini of Iran? Do we allow movie critics to determine which movies we see? If not to these people, then to whom do we turn? What choice mechanisms do we employ? Will the decisions made under any other choice mechanism be any better, on average, than the choices of many individuals?

Freedom is the dispersion of decision-making power. To the extent that each of us has some of that power, then the power that each has is limited. In a discussion of Adam Smith, Friedrich Hayek observed:

It would scarcely be too much to claim that the main merit of individualism that he [Adam Smith] and his contemporaries advocated is that it is a system under which bad men can do least harm. It is a social system which does not depend for its functioning on our finding good men for running it, or on all men becoming better than they are now, but which makes use of men in all of their given variety and complexity, sometimes good and sometimes bad, sometimes intelligent and more often stupid. Their aim was a system under which it should be possible to grant freedom to all, instead of restricting it, as their French contemporaries wished, to "the good and the wise."[3]

Individualism is a social philosophy of freedom. If this philosophy does not have broad-based application, freedom is necessarily restricted. To the extent that we rely on highly detailed rules to guide human behavior, we deny freedom to many.

EQUALITY UNDER LAW

When Lincoln spoke of the equality of men, he was not naively suggesting that all men are in fact the same. Nor was he intimating that he perceived men to be equal in all or even the most important respects. He no doubt had advisers whom he valued over others. Similarly, each of us can perceive the distinguishing characteristics of people. Some we like; some we dislike. For some—those whom we love and cherish—we might even lay down our lives, for others—particularly those faraway whose names we do not know—we might sacrifice very little to ensure their continued good health or even life. Men are not the same, objectively or subjectively.

What, then, do Lincoln and others mean when they talk about the "equality of men"? Two reasonable answers come to mind. First, individuals may differ drastically in capabilities, but they are still accepted and treated as equals by their Creator in the same way that most parents accept and treat each of their children as equals. Parents may foster differences in their offspring by allowing them to seek, within broad boundaries, their own individual ways in life; still, they treat all of their children impartially as if they were equal. Second, "equality of men" may mean that under the law justice is blind to human differences and the same rules apply equally to all people.

This book is not concerned with God's view of mankind. Little can be said of it beyond that which already has. In any case, God can fend for himself. Our concern is with human institutions, agreed *to* and created *by* people to serve the purposes *of* people. This must have been Lincoln's central concern at Gettysburg when he raised the issue of equality, for the Civil War was fought in part over the proposition that all people—black and white—must be treated the same under law so they can be equally human—that is, so they can be different. It was not fought to make people equal in fact, to redo what God had failed to do, to provide equal opportunity, or to make incomes equal. The Civil War and many of the civil rights struggles that occurred in our lifetime were waged simply to ensure that each person counts the same under the law.

The notion of equality under law elevates the importance of the individual not because each person is somehow indispensable to society—virtually everyone can be replaced—but because each person, in spite of surface attributes, counts for one, distinguishable legal entity with rights separable from everyone else's. The individual himself, because he happens to exist, counts for something. That is what is meant by "primacy of the individual," as distinct from the primacy of a personality such as that possessed by Ronald Reagan or Jane Fonda.

Why should individuals be treated equally under the law? That important and intriguing question in social philosophy is not altogether easy to answer. In answering the question, we may simply assert, as many people do, that the individual is important because he is a child of God. Fortunately, we can say more. By treating each person as equal under the law, we in effect give each individual the same rights legally held by all other persons. Hence, no person can enlist the law and the power of the state to make himself dominant over part or all of the rest of the population. In this sense, the law is blind to the individual's ambitions.

Equality under the law, and the philosophy of individualism that legal equality inspires, is—to repeat a theme of this book—an effective social means of dispersing power in the economy and society. It is a way of saying, "No one has the power to coerce another." If one person has that right, then under a legal order in which people are treated equally, all persons have that right. If all have the right to coerce, no one is then free of coercion from others. In such an anarchistic world, law would serve no purpose; and life, to use the stark terms of Thomas

Hobbes, the seventeenth-century philosopher, might very well be "solitary, poor, nasty, brutish, and short." According to Hobbes, there would be "no property . . . no *Mine* and *Thine* distinct, but only to be every man's that he can get, and for so long as he can keep it."[4]

The purpose of laws that give prominence to individuals is to foster freedom by dispersing power and by handing over to each person some legally permissible realm of activity. As John Locke wrote many years ago,

> The end of law is not to abolish or restrain but to preserve and enlarge freedom; for in all the states of created beings capable of laws, where there is no law, there is no freedom. For liberty is to be free from restraint and violence of others, which cannot be where there is no law . . . For who could be free, when every man's human might domineer over him?[5]

Equality under the law is a legal principle that adds an element of fairness to the treatment of people. We usually consider parlor games fair only when the rules are not *intentionally* designed to benefit any particular player or group of players. The rules may benefit one player—someone has to win—but the critical point is that they are not written to give that particular player, as defined, say, by a name of a personality, an advantage over the other players. When all players agree to the rules before the game is begun, the outcome of the game is usually deemed fair. Indeed, the fairness of the game is usually judged not by its outcome—the outcome has no particular moral content—but rather by the way in which the rules of the game are devised and by the extent to which the rules of the game are explicitly or implicitly accepted beforehand.[6]

In establishing a social order, we need general consent to the rules of the game, or else the order that is erected cannot remain stable. As Ortega y Gasset said, "Order is not a pressure imposed upon society from without, but an equilibrium which is set up from within." To achieve order, we must look for very general principles of organization that, by their nature, can elicit meaningful consent. The important question is Are there any principles that will gain the necessary social acceptance? The principle of equality under the law is a prime candidate. Granted that equality under the law, on which political and economic freedoms are founded, may work to the economic advantage of some people, it is still one of those principles that tends to achieve considerable consensus. It is not perfect—no rule will ever be that. On the other hand, it can be construed as just because of its purpose, not because of its results. The results of the principle of equality under the law are consistent with its purpose—that it keep people free. Different results occur partly because people employ their freedom differently.

Equality under the law does not imply that each person is given the same property rights or the same income or the same abilities to operate within the context of the law. It simply means that the law will be equally applied; the property rights of all people, regardless of how much property a person owns, will be protected in the same way by the legal system. A rich person may have more property than a poor person and, hence, may secure more quantitative benefits from the protective legal system than the poor person. This does not mean, however, that the laws are applied with favoritism for the rich. Again, the application, not the particular consequences, of the law, is the standard by which its fairness is judged under the philosophy of individualism, a philosophy that, as indicated above, must underpin a free society.

COMPLEX PHENOMENA AND MARKET EXCHANGES

The free market (or free enterprise) system has, as I have attempted to show, a strong philosophical foundation; it protects freedom by elevating the dignity of the individual to social prominence. The system, however, also has a firm pragmatic foundation: it works. It is really the only system that effectively and efficiently serves the desires and preferences of a diverse humanity.

Each individual is unique, not fully duplicated anywhere else. Therefore, each individual possesses considerable knowledge that is not and cannot be fully known by anyone else—by government or by any group of people. Each individual has preferences—needs and wants—of which only he can be cognizant at any point in time; he also has a unique capacity to envision new wants when old ones have been partially or fully satisfied. The individual knows, within limits, what gives him gain and causes him pain; and he knows this before any of his actions are revealed to others. He can understand the subjective basis for his actions before he acts; others can only observe his actions after the fact and guess at his motivation by reflecting on their own, *different* preferences. Each individual has abilities to work and play, to grasp new thoughts and retain old ones, to love and to hate, to care and be cared for, to create new images and destroy worn ones, to eat and sleep, to live and die. The suggestion that a human being is productive only when working certainly presents a myopic view of human circumstance; such a view ignores so many dimensions of our abilities. Each of us is barely able to comprehend his or her own diverse abilities; how can we possibly know the full range of abilities of people whom we have never and can never meet.

In addition, only the individual can comprehend (albeit imperfectly) the trade-offs that he is willing to make between the things he wants now and in the future. Only the individual can understand before the fact what he is willing to forgo for a product as simple as an apple; only the individual knows under what circumstances he prefers to eat an apple.

We may think that we know a great deal about human behavior when we observe people buying apples, but there is so much that we can never know. We cannot know, for example, the cost of an apple to an individual. To be sure, we can see that an individual pays so many cents for an apple, but we must observe him in the act of trade before we know that he even likes apples, much less is willing to bear the cost of buying the apple. The true cost of anything is the most highly valued opportunity that an individual forgoes in buying that good. The price of an apple tells us something about its cost, but not very much. It suggests to us some of the other things an individual may have to forgo to buy the apple, but it does not tell us exactly what is given up for the apple. The cost is the value of the opportunity not taken, and there is no way that we can objectively observe the value of what another individual fails to do.

The purchase of an apple appears on the surface to be a relatively simple act, uniform across people who are in the market for apples. But appearances are deceiving. The late Frank Knight, mentor of so many present-day free market economists, used to puzzle his students at the University of Chicago with the elementary question, "What is an apple?" If called on, we can all identify an apple, but once we reflect seriously on the puzzle, we begin to understand that apples are different things to different people. Knight used to tell his students that although apples have a concrete identity in objective reality, it may be more accurate to say that people consume "images of apples" rather than just "apples." The latter suggests a uniformity in consumption, that simply does not exist. We all buy apples for slightly different purposes and eat them (or throw them or bob for them or display them) in slightly different circumstances. The circumstances of consumption must be different because we are different. If we know so little about other people's motivation when they purchase and consume an apple, just think how little we know about people's decisions to buy a new car, to go to college, to rear children, to go on vacation, or to chart the course of a career.

The technology of efficient production of most products usually dictates that people must specialize in one aspect of production, which means that no one person knows how to produce the entire product. It is doubtful that any one person at Texas Instruments knows how to build a complete hand calculator. There is, indeed, someone in that organization who is able to explain the workings of the hand calculator, but he is not necessarily able, by himself, to assemble a hand calculator. It is even more unlikely that such a person knows how to make all of the components, or assemble all of the materials that go into the components, or transform the materials into components for a hand calculator. Information is diffused and seldom controlled by any one person— and must necessarily be so in a complex society.

We are constitutionally ignorant about what other people want and do. That stark fact must humble anyone or any group who thinks that an entire economy can sensibly be centrally organized to serve the ends of a heterogeneous population. Social planners may think they can effectively and efficiently plan an entire economy to serve the ends of the people for whom the planning is done. However, their immense ignorance about people will inevitably lead to failure. Surveys of people's wants provide very limited and distorted information about their relative values, their "needs" and "wants." As a later chapter discusses in more detail, democracy (the voting mechanism) is a very poor means for determining people's preferences. Votes can be cast either for or against a limited number of proposals offered in referenda, but votes remain extraordinarily poor devices for registering the *intensity* of different people's wants and desires. Furthermore, why would we want to rely on the cumbersome procedures of democracy to determine how many toothpicks or bow ties to produce?

Many opponents of the free enterprise system think that the markets, the profits, and the prices that emerge from the free exchanges of individuals are unnecessary—the extraneous trappings of an oppressive system that serves no useful purpose and that, therefore, can be replaced by some brand of socialist control. They imagine that markets can be supplanted by a bureaucracy sufficiently elaborate to plan with reasonable effectiveness and tolerable efficiency the economic activity of an entire country. Furthermore, they think that the organizational structure can fully account for the preferences of the larger community of individuals that the organization is intended to serve.

In the 1930s, 1940s, and 1950s, there was a great deal of scholarly interest among economists on the question, Can socialism replace capitalism and achieve the same results? One readily accepted answer was that socialism would not be inefficient so long as the planners attempted to maximize profits. These scholars overlooked some very basic points. They forgot that the movement from free markets under capitalism to controlled markets under socialism implies a radical shift in property rights and, hence, a major change in the incentive structure. The shift from free markets to controlled markets also means a shift from private decision making to collective decision making, which requires the use of the slow, inflexible democratic process.[7] Even to those who did not understand the complicated mathematics employed in the debate, an important point was obvious. Socialism cannot conceptually or realistically replace capitalism without a decline in economic efficiency—the ability of the economic system to satisfy the wants of individuals (as opposed to the wants of planners).

Organizational structures are important to economic activity. They enable people to come together for a common purpose, to produce a good, to provide a setting for worship, or to give to a worthy cause. They pool a great many talents, draw on much specialized information, and provide the individuals involved with the incentives they need to produce and to serve the common purpose. New forms of organizational structure are, perhaps, among the most important inventions of the twentieth century; without them, we certainly would not have been able to take advantage of the vast cost savings available to large-scale operations. However, the organization of people into one hierarchal structure has technological limitations. There are limits to how many people can be brought together before the links between the people at the bottom and those at the top of the structure become so weak that people in the organization work less effectively and incentives and costs savings evaporate.

As the areas covered by a given organization are extended, as they must be extended in socialism, decision-making power can be delegated to a larger and larger number of "technocrats," a phrase made popular by John Kenneth Galbraith.[8] However, as an organization expands, greater and greater responsibility is placed on the people at the top of the hierarchy; greater and greater reliance is placed on the limited intelligence of the people at the top for effective decisions governing the coordination and production of the people at the bottom. (If this upward shift of responsibility does not occur, we must wonder why the hierarchal structure was needed in the first place.) There is only so much that any one person or group or persons can know, and there is only so much effective responsibility that any one person or group of persons can assume.

At some point, an expansion of an organization to manage the economy pushes the people at the top beyond their "levels of competence." The only way they can effectively manage the economy at all is to reduce the managerial problem to the limits of their own abilities. Normally they limit the number and diversity of wants served by the organization, inevitably imposing their own preferences on those members of society that they are supposed to serve and treating us all as groups and classes—as though we are cattle to be herded about for their purposes. Hence, control, which implies loss of freedom, goes hand in hand with the collectivization of economic activity.

Walter Lippmann made this fundamental point with more punch: "The generation to which we belong is now learning from experience what happens when man retreats from freedom to a coercive organization of their affairs. Though they promise themselves a more abundant life, they must in practice renounce it; as the organizational direction increases, the variety of ends must give way to uniformity. That is the nemesis of the planned society and the authoritarian principle in human affairs."[9] Hayek has repeatedly warned that failure to understand the limitations of individual knowledge inevitably leads down what he calls "the road to serfdom":

> The fundamental attitude of true individualism is one of humility toward processes by which mankind has achieved things which have not been designed or understood by any individual and are indeed greater than individual minds. The great question at this moment is whether man's mind will be allowed to continue to grow as part of this

process or whether human reason is to place itself in chains of its own making.

What individualism teaches is that society is greater than the individual only insofar as he is free. Insofar as it is controlled or directed, it is limited to the powers of the individual minds which control or direct it. If the presumption of the modern mind, which will not respect anything that is not consciously controlled by individual reason, does not learn in time where to stop, we may, as Edmund Burke warned us, "be well assured that everything about us will dwindle by degree, until at length our concerns are shrunk to the dimensions of our minds."[10]

Some social critics overly impressed with modern technology fantasize that markets can be supplanted by computers. Computers, they explain, can compute the market demands and supplies of everything from automobiles to lollipops; they can determine market-clearing prices and send out elaborate orders on exactly how much each firm must produce. Computers, so the argument goes, will determine the market-clearing quantities, of, say, automobiles of a certain style and size that a given firm like General Motors will produce. They will also issue orders to all of the suppliers of the 6,256 parts that General Motors needs and to all of the suppliers of all of the basic materials that go into the production of the parts that go into the automobiles. In addition, these computers will distribute orders to firms that will transport all of the materials, parts, and finished cars to ensure that everything gets to its destination. Income will also be distributed according to the dictates of a computer program that is deemed "fair" by some democratic decision-making process. This will enable consumers to buy the exact number of cars produced. Furthermore, all of these orders relating to a given style automobile will be made compatible with all other orders relating to the millions of other goods and services produced in the economy.

To suggest that any computer or combination of computers has, or will have, the technical capacity to accomplish such a task is pure nonsense. However, there is a much more basic reason why a computer cannot allocate resources, parts, and final products among all competing uses: no computer can get the necessary information on what different individuals want and need. True, consumers do demand a given product, say, a certain model automobile. But how, outside the market process, can the government know what consumers want? Can the government simply ask consumers what they want? Many have only a vague understanding of their preferences. Many are in the market looking for information on types of products that they could want. In other words, the determination of wants and of market-clearing prices and quantities are not always independent events that can be separated by government surveys. Furthermore, social scientists know that there is often a big gulf between consumers' answers to surveys questions and what they actually do when confronted with real choices involving real prices and the immediate circumstances of consumption.

If the government cannot get the necessary information, how can it determine market-clearing prices and quantities? How can it give the computer its instructions? An important conclusion is obvious: the market serves the purpose of gathering and disseminating meaningful information on people's preferences and abilities; it serves a social function that cannot be performed very effectively—and still provide for individual freedom—in any other way. Furthermore, the market has a tremendous capacity, albeit imperfect, to adjust to changes in individual preferences and abilities that cannot be anticipated. In short, the particular outcomes of a market are the result of a process that, as Hayek has repeatedly emphasized, is the consequence of human action but not of human design.[11] We must "design" the framework for the market, letting the particular outcomes remain open issues to be settled within this framework.

The market is indeed a mysterious social mechanism that allocates resources and things we want in spite of our tremendous ignorance about the individuals involved in that process. If it were not for our ignorance, the case for the free market would be strong, but not nearly so strong as it is. Paradoxically, as society becomes more sophisticated, our reliance on the market must become progressively greater. "The more men know, the smaller the share of that knowledge becomes that any one mind can absorb. The more civilized we become, the more relatively ignorant must each individual be of the facts on which the working of his civilization depends. The very division of knowledge increases the necessary ignorance of the individual of most of this knowledge."[12] The division of knowledge increases the need for a decentralized decision-making system—the market.

"POOR JIMMY"

Jimmy Carter entered the presidency with the respect of much of the country. His background as a peanut farmer from a small town in Georgia contributed mightily to his image of respectability, forthrightness, and honesty. He led us all to believe that his sense of fair play and his willingness to work, with humility, at the job of being president would help solve our pressing social and economic problems.

By the 1980 election campaign, the tide of public opinion had shifted dramatically. President Carter had become the butt of numerous not-so-kind jokes concerning the relative intelligence of Miss Lillian's two sons. Speakers around the country noted that Jimmy Carter was the first president whose popularity ratings were exceeded by the prime rate and the inflation rate.

Like his immediate predecessor, President Carter was often characterized as a man who could barely stumble and bumble his way off helicopters, much less guide the country toward economic and social stability. His record on domestic matters especially seemed so bad that some people grew accustomed to thinking sympathetically of the most powerful leader of the free world as "poor Jimmy."

Why did this shift in the public's attitude occur? Why do we seem to elect with such regularity leaders who fail so miserably at the task of guiding the economy? Rather than improving conditions, our presidents appear to muck up just about everything—inflation, unemployment, productivity, and personal income.

The problem in the late 1970s was not Jimmy Carter's intelligence—he has, no doubt, above average intelligence. Nor was the problem his integrity—he generally meant well. The fact of the matter is that the job of being president has risen in complexity to the point that it is now beyond the competence of any mortal—Carter or Reagan—to handle intelligently. Our presidents are now bound to fail because we have come to expect and demand far too much of our government and its head.

Today, the president of the United States is expected to cope with a bewildering array of subjects, any one of which can tax the competence of even the brightest among us: unemployment, energy, inflation, drought, volcanoes, nuclear power, the defense of the nation, deregulation of the trucking industry, regulation of a host of other industries, the value-added tax, equal employment opportunities, the draft, the money supply, a budget measured not by pages but by pounds, social security, hazards in the work place, urban riots, illegal immigrants, and equal rights amendments. And the president must be able to understand and appreciate all the obvious and subtle conflicts, trade-offs, interrelationships, and downright contradictions inherent in the smorgasbord of government policies that flow incessantly from the federal bureaucracy.

Surely, the president must often feel buffeted by events and the immense pressures brought to bear on his office by special interest groups that span the political spectrum, each claiming that government must do something to help them. All the while, the president must keep one ear cocked, ready to hear the latest word on what is happening to our foreign policy.

No man or woman, with the best of help and intentions, can do what we now ask of our president. Until voters realize that the power of the government to do good is limited, we will very likely witness a series of one-term presidents and inconsistent policies that will keep us on an economic roller coaster and will cause us to question the competence of our political leaders.

THE EMERGING MARKET

We may know little about the specific content of the behavior of individuals we have never met, but that does not mean we know nothing. We can speculate on the broad boundaries of human behavior. We know that people have their own preferences and abilities and that they know much about themselves that we cannot hope to know. We also know that they, like us, are motivated to pursue whatever they imperfectly believe is in their own interest. If given freedom of action, they will search out ways of satisfying their wants and needs—as they define them. That may mean they will do many things for themselves, but it also means that most will seek others with whom they can cooperate in production and with whom they share common interests—as they define their common interests. We know in addition that the pursuit of private interests leads people to engage in trades that, when free, tend to be mutually beneficial. Perhaps the most important contribution to the study of mankind made by economists is the simple demonstration that free trades are profitable to both parties: no one gains at the expense of another when free exchanges occur. Aside from instances of mistakes or fraud, which cannot be condoned in a free market system, trades lead to social betterment, as the participants to the trades define betterment. *Free* trades would simply not occur unless this were true. To deny exchanges is to deny improvement.

Markets for goods and services emerge not because of orders issued by some central authority, but because the individuals who participate in markets want to be in them. Markets can become quite complicated processes involving money, prices, credit, middlemen, large- and small-scale production, transportation networks, and a variety of organizational forms. They are largely anarchistic in the sense that detailed external control is absent, but they are a form of "self-generating order" resulting from free individuals doing free things.

When people find a better way of doing something or a better buy, they are free to adjust within the context of the law that applies equally to all. When markets are free, people can exploit profitable opportunities left unexploited by others.

Competition is the social hallmark of freedom, but it is a social serendipity arising from the fundamental positions that individuals, although often misguided, are the best judges of what they should do with their lives and that power should be dispersed among many individuals. Where power is concentrated in the hands of a few, there is little or no freedom (except for those who have the power), no competition, and none of the benefits that can accrue from competition. Free market economists cannot tolerate the concentration of economic power in the hands of so-called private individuals any more than they can tolerate the concentration of economic and political power in the hands of the government. Power is anathema to the free enterprise system and must be opposed because it basically conflicts with individual freedom.

Markets emerge spontaneously. They feed on differences, for differences are the basis of so many trades. When two people differ in their relative evaluations of the products they produce, both can trade, each giving up that product he likes relatively less in exchange for that product he likes relatively more. Otherwise neither could gain from the trade. If we were all alike in preferences and abilities—identical—there would be no basis for so many of the markets we observe in the real world.[13] In short, markets make it possible for us to retain our individuality. At the same time, they give us the incentive we need to produce efficiently and to serve the general good by directing our efforts toward helping others. An oft-quoted passage from Adam Smith's *Wealth of Nations* is particularly appropriate here: "By directing that industry in such a manner as its produce may be of greatest value, he intends only his own gain, and he is in this . . . led by an invisible hand to promote an end which was no part of his intentions. Nor is it always worse for the society that it was not part of. By pursuing his own interests he frequently promotes that of society more effectively than when he really intends to promote it."[14]

COMMON OBJECTIONS TO THE FREE MARKET SYSTEM

Criticisms of the free market (or free enterprise) system are legion. They emanate from almost all sectors of society, including the business community; they are given dramatic emphasis by the attention they receive in the daily media. This chapter concludes by considering several of the more prominent and frequently voiced objections (printed in italics below) to the social system that, I have argued, makes freedom and action possible.

The free market system is founded on greed—the profit motive. The system deifies the almighty dollar, undermining other social values. Greed is a sin that needs to be tempered, not glorified, by the social-economic system.

The free market system fundamentally concerns freedom in general, not just the freedom to make a buck. Under the system people are given the social space to pursue what they view as their own interest; they are not told to maximize profits or anything else. What they maximize is, within the broad limits of the law, up to them. There is nothing in the free enterprise system that prevents people from pursuing goals that have little or nothing to do with money, from being ethical, or from being altruistic. If people cannot choose, within limits, what they pursue, then freedom has little meaning.

People who have not read Adam Smith's classic work believe that he sanctified laissez-faire capitalism and totally ignored human values and motivations not captured in money. This view could not be more distorted. Before writing *The Wealth of Nations*, Smith wrote another book that is perhaps more important in the development of our intellectual history. In *The Theory of Moral Sentiments*, Smith delineated what he considered to be the necessary moral foundation of society. One gets the distinct impression that *Moral Sentiments* was meant to be a companion volume to *The Wealth of Nations* and that Smith was convinced that any economic system must be founded on moral behavior—an ethical code of conduct that guides people in their personal and financial dealings with others. He stressed the importance of the "virtues of prudence, justice, and beneficence." Without an ethical code, any economic system may very well destroy itself, Smith wrote:

> Without the restraint which this principle [or impartial spectator] imposes, every passion would upon occasion, rush head-long, if I may say so, to its own gratification. Anger would follow the suggestion of its own fury; fear those of its own violent agitation. Regard to no time or place would induce vanity to refrain from the loudest and most impertinent ostentation; or voluptuousness from the most open, indecent, and scandalous indulgence. Respect for what are, or for what ought to be, or for what, upon certain conditions, would be, the sentiments of other people is the sole principle which, upon most occasions, overawes all those mutinous and turbulent passions into that tone and temper which the impartial spectator can enter into and sympathize with.[15]

If we as a society lose our moral foundation—our sense of justice, prudence, and fair play—then surely our economic system will operate less effectively. Our sense of fairness breeds trust. In the absence of trust, many mutually beneficial transactions will never be made because the costs of achieving agreement will escalate. True, the free enterprise system is founded on a strong legal system, but it must also be based on the everyday notion of "goodwill" because the legal system cannot be so pervasive in our lives that it can tell us in every instance what is right or wrong, legitimate or illegitimate, and just or unjust. From a continuing study of business contractual relationships, legal scholar Stewart Macaulay concludes that

> in all of these societies—which differ so greatly in social structure, culture, and political and economic ideology—the picture looks much the same. Industrial managers seldom litigate to solve disputes about contracts, preferring to use other techniques or dispute avoidance and settlement. Perhaps the surprising thing is that anyone would expect the use of contract litigation to be other than rare and the influence of contract to be anything other than but indirect. Few, for example, would expect the process of divorce as it is expressed in statutes and cases to have much influence on ongoing marriage relationships.[16]

The implication of Macaulay's analysis is that contracts have meaning to the parties involved because of trust and ongoing economic dependence.

Moral behavior must always be an open issue in a free enterprise system. Those of us who are proponents of the system cannot ignore instances of private injustice and corruption, pretending that they are of no concern. We must object and object strongly. However, we must be very cautious about turning to government to remedy observed injustices. If dealings in private markets are corrupt, there is no assurance that government, which is run by representatives of the larger society, will not reflect the private corruption. Indeed, the corrupt will surely want to use government's coercive power to further their own corrupt ends.

The free enterprise–profit system means that some people are allowed to make money off others.

Profit has become a four-letter word. Marx argued that profit was unearned income and suggested that it had no socially redeeming value. Many people today seem to agree with Marx. With the attention given to the profits of oil companies in recent years, people have surmised that most big companies earn fantastic rates of return on their investment—30 or 40 percent. This perception of business profits is, of course, grossly distorted and can be dealt with by referring to the facts. However, to reiterate a point made earlier, in a free society both parties to a trade "profit" by it. One reason businesses get such a bum rap when it comes to profit is that there is no way to cacluate the profits consumers make off trades with businesses. The profits of consumers are largely subjective. When the media announce that, for example, Gulf Oil made $110 million in profits during the first quarter of the year, they cannot follow with an estimate of how much consumers gained by Gulf Oil's existence. The listener is left with the lopsided impression that Gulf Oil has served only its interests and not also those of the larger society.

In interpreting profits, we must understand that they are made because someone or some organization perceived a profitable opportunity, that is, a way of providing consumers with something they wanted at a cheaper cost. Profits are often viewed as a consequence of a zero-sum game: what one person gets, another loses. However, more often than not, they are the result of a positive-sum game, a game that benefits both parties to the trade. Therefore, the pursuit of profit leads to an expansion, not a contraction, of the national income level.

Proponents of the free market system assume individuals know what they want and are able to calculate their best interests very precisely. However, human beings are not machines and cannot be counted on to operate as machines.

It is indeed true that people make mistakes, are subject to psychological quirks, are sometimes paranoid and often neurotic, and are—as frequently as not—stupid. Despite these behavioral patterns, economists are prone to postulate that individuals are *rational* when it comes to market transactions—that individuals know what they want and are capable of consistently pursuing their wants. The purpose of this assumption is not to describe the behavior of real people fully but to develop a model of behavior that will enable economists to make predictions about behavior. The usefulness of these models is limited by the descriptive relevance of the assumption of rational behavior. Frank Knight observed that practically all of life's problems concern how we should use our resources to achieve desired results: that is, how we should utilize our resources economically. Knight pointed out that "the first question in regard to scientific economics is this question of how far life is rational." However, Knight also questioned how far life's problems can be reduced "to the form of using given means to achieve given ends" and suggested that "life is at bottom an exploration in the field of values . . . We strive to 'know ourselves,' to find out our real wants, more than to get what we want."[17]

Much of the professional stature of economists rests on their ability to predict future events in free markets. However, the case for the free market itself does not depend on the predictive ability of economists. Rather, the basis of the case for the free market is our ignorance of what people will do with freedom. The free market allows people to make mistakes, as they surely will, and to adjust, as they see fit, when they learn they have erred. It allows them to find themselves. Without freedom it is doubtful that people can really know their wants or themselves.

The claim that many people do not know what is good for them is often heard. Of course, that is true; but it does not follow that others are better judges of what they *should* want. Officials in Washington have meager information on the circumstances of people in Six Mile, South Carolina, and are very poor judges of what they should do with their lives. What appear to be psychological quirks to people in Washington may be rational acts to people in Six Mile, and vice versa. Either freedom means freedom of individual action, or it means nothing.

If left free to do and buy what we want, many people will drink booze, go to pornographic movies, enlist the attentions of prostitutes, attend the services of religious quacks, eat too much sugar, smoke too many cigarettes—in general, go to hell.

Freedom requires each of us to assume at least a modicum of humility when it comes to judging what is best for others. It requires that we be extraordinarily tolerant of what others do with their lives. We, perhaps, have an obligation to give our best advice to friends and loved ones. We must, in this way and to this extent, be our brothers' keeper; our social system depends on these kinds of personal inter-dependencies. However, if we assume a moral obligation to force other people, with whom we have little or no contact, to behave the way we think they should, we can destroy the freedom they *and* we have. Any political system that allows us to tell others what they should do with their lives can be used by others to restrict what we do with our lives. By restricting the political power of government to control people's lives, we surrender some of our freedom to control others; we gain the freedom to be left alone and to do, within broad boundaries, as we wish.

Granted, certain extreme cases of free market transactions cannot be tolerated by a civilized people. A number of years ago, for example, it was *rumored* that one could buy a pornographic film that showed the actual killing and butchering of a woman. The murder was, of course, a crime. Further, the film could not have been sold legally because it would have been made in connection with a crime. Legalistic consideration aside, the relevant question for our purposes is If the film had been made and if people had been willing to pay to see it, should it have been allowed on the free market? Should (or does) free enterprise economics condone such free transactions? Hardly. Freedom, by its nature, contains the inherent risk of abuse. There are extreme instances of abuse that must be contained by collective, governmental means; otherwise, the public's confidence and acceptance of freedom as a social norm can be undermined. The central message of free enterprise economics is very simple: We must bend over backwards and then some in allowing people to do as they wish, tolerating much that we personally find objectionable, but that does not mean we should allow ourselves to return all the way to the jungle.

The free market system is based on property rights, and property rights confer considerable benefits on property owners.

There is no way of denying that millionaires absorb a significant part of national income. And it is not easy to justify the income of some of these people—those who do little but clip coupons from inherited bonds. On the other hand, there are several points that need to be kept in mind when evaluating the distribution of the country's wealth and income. First, the number of people who receive unearned income is relatively inconsequential. Most of the people who receive high incomes earned them in free markets by providing something of value to people free to buy or not to buy.

Second, discussions of the distribution of the nation's wealth tend to focus on the physical wealth people own. However, in a free society people effectively own themselves, and the property that they own in themselves is typically far more valuable than their material belongings. In other words, total property is more evenly distributed in a free society than one would surmise by looking at the distribution of physical property. Besides, the basis of wealth, measured in so many dollars, lies not in "things" but in the imagination of people who have a vision of the future and the wants of others in that future that they can satisfy. This must be so since the value of physical property held today is necessarily the present discounted value of all earnings anticipated in the future. Today's wealth must, therefore, be counterbalanced by consumers' demand for future goods.

Third, most of the physical wealth that exists today did not exist fifty years ago. It was created through the inventive power of people, using their human capital. Similarly, most of the wealth that will exist fifty years from now does not exist today. It, too, will be created by the inventive powers of imaginative people. The creators of wealth will benefit directly from it. On the other hand, free trades must always and everywhere be beneficial to producers *and* consumers.

Fourth, equal distribution of a country's physical wealth is not always socially desirable, not even for the poor. If we adopt a policy of distributing wealth equally, we will destroy people's incentives to produce. People will gain nothing by producing; they will know that anytime their wealth exceeds the wealth of others, a portion will be taken away. This will result not only in a leveling of wealth but also in a reduction in the total amount of wealth. The poor can be better off by having the wealth unevenly distributed than by having a much lower quantity of wealth equally distributed.

Fifth, people's abilities to produce differ. Those with greater abilities tend to have higher incomes, by definition. Again, we should remember that trades in free markets tend to benefit both parties to the trades. People with lower abilities tend to benefit from others' greater abilities. Would the disadvantaged of the country be better or worse off if, for some reason, the gifted disappeared? On average, the disadvantaged would be worse off.

Sixth, many proponents of income redistribution through government romantically assume that the democratic process can be opened up for the sole purpose of taking from the "rich" and giving to the "poor." That is what "collectivization of charity" is supposed to mean. The problem with this position is that we must wonder why high- (or even middle-) income groups would not, when transfers are permitted, use their political power to redistribute income the other way, from the poor to the rich (or why the middle-income group that dominates the political process would not use its special political position to redistribute income from both the lowest- and highest-income groups to itself). Casual and detailed studies of government operations suggests that in an open-ended welfare state, the poor can be victims as often or more often than they are the beneficiaries of state-organized redistributive efforts.

Still, there are some people so disadvantaged that they are unable to operate at all in a free market. We cannot always count on private charitable activity to help many of these people. Free enterprise economics does not rule out all government assistance to the disadvantaged. However, it warns that we must be careful in using government to transfer wealth and income. Such transfers can reduce people's incentive to produce and their generosity toward others. If we go very far in using the power of government to redistribute wealth and income, we can make the relative poor of today *and* tomorrow worse, not better, off.

The free market system is founded on individualistic behavior. The system does not allow, is even philosophically opposed to, group or collective action.

This criticism, although frequently voiced, is off-base and misdirected. Nothing in the free market system conflicts with concerted action by a family or group of people for their common good. In a free society people can join with whomever they like and do, within the bounds of the law, whatever they like. Freedom includes the freedom to join and leave groups at will.

Some arguments suggest that many people who share a common interest cannot, without governmental assistance, collectively pursue their common interest. The argument is often applied to large groups in which each person is relatively insignificant. Each person in a very large group can reason that his contributing or failing to contribute to the common effort makes no difference. Hence, no individual has an incentive to participate in the group's activities. Each individual, so the argument goes, becomes a "free rider." The result is that little or nothing is done by people who have a collective want but no private incentive to achieve it.

As an example, envision a neighborhood with an entrance way littered with paper and overgrown with weeds. Each person in the neighborhood wants to see the entrance way cleaned up; however, no one is likely to do anything because others are not doing anything. Each has an incentive to clean up a portion of the entrance way, but not the entire area. The result is that all have to endure the unsightly mess at the entrance to their neighborhood. Again, we must be very careful not to jump to the easily drawn conclusion that government must, in such instances, take action. First, neighborhoods can be organized to clean up their own messes. Second, sometimes the cost of collective action to the group outweighs the benefits. Third, when government is employed to accomplish group objectives, we often move from a state in which there are free riders to a state in which there are "forced riders." The shift is not necessarily an improvement. More is said on this argument below; here I merely emphasize that group action is expected and observed under free market systems.

Freedom has often been touted as a standard for judging the results of individual actions. If the individual is free to do as he wishes, then the results must be good; if he is not free, then the results must be "bad." Although useful as a social criterion, freedom is often but not always easy to justify on the basis of results. Free people sometimes do things that are objectionable to large numbers of people. Incomes, which are the results of free market transactions, depend on effort, but they also depend on the initial distribution of property, inheritance, and the toss of the die in the distribution of human genes. Further, inequality of wealth can be increased by the use of resources; those who have greater quantities of wealth are, because of their high incomes, better able to reinvest the income generated by the wealth they possess.

Looking at these stark facts, Frank Knight concluded that the ethical significance of the results of free markets is inextricably tied to the ethical context within which those results are achieved: "It is simply and briefly that freedom is itself an ethical category."[18] Freedom allows for mutually beneficial trades of property (given the morality of the initial distribution). It permits improvements (not perfection), by which is meant that results are judged by the context within which the results are achieved. The criterion employed by economists to judge the "efficiency" of market results is (contrary to what economists may contend) highly normative. The concept of efficiency is predicated on individual evaluations of goods and services and the extent to which people are free to express those evaluations. The use of efficiency, like the use of freedom, is ethically grounded. Many objections to the free market can be disputed. We can show where and to what extent many of the objections are misguided or actually reflect one person's interest in controlling others. We cannot hope to address all of the objections here. Even if we could, in the final analysis, for free markets to exist, people must value freedom for itself. This means that we must allow, within broad limits, each individual to do what he or she wants, that we must assert his or her ethical right to do so. That is the bottom line.

The Collectivist Mentality

The man of systems . . . seems to imagine that he can arrange the different members of a great society with as much ease as the hand arranges the different pieces upon the chess-board; he does not consider pieces upon the chess-board have no other principle of motion besides that which the hand impresses upon them; but that, in the great chess-board of human society, every single piece has a principle of motion of its own, altogether different from that which the legislature might choose to impress upon it.

Adam Smith
The Theory of Moral Sentiments

CHAPTER 4

During the spring and summer of 1979, the United States experienced another energy crisis. The crisis seemed real, not contrived by OPEC; it appeared to many that we were on the brink of running out of oil. During the first six months of the year, the price of gasoline rose by 40 percent or more. There were scattered reports of price gouging by filling station owners who more than doubled their prices. Fines and criminal charges were leveled against several owners.

Almost all service stations were closing on weekends and evenings, and some owners were filling tanks only by appointment. Many were setting either minimum or maximum purchase amounts. Still, lines of cars, stretching for blocks and even miles, formed around the gasoline stations that were open. Fights broke out among people waiting in line. When one Washington area lady broke line, the infuriated man behind her put his gas cap on her car, locked it, and then drove off, taking the key with him. On a few occasions angry customers even fired shots at one another or at service station owners, reminding one of the words of the famous social philosopher Al Capone: "You can do more with a kind word and a gun than you can with a kind word alone."[1]

Meanwhile, Congress was playing a tragicomedy in economic policy formulation. When service station lines formed earlier in California than in other parts of the country, Governor Jerry Brown declared that the Department of Energy's formula for allocating fuel supplies was "unfair" and failed to account for the influx of people into and the economic growth of his state. In May he made a trip to Washington for an urgent meeting with the president, from whom he got a commitment for additional gasoline supplies. In June Las Vegas and other tourist areas dependent on the motoring public experienced serious drops in business because people feared they would be stranded. Politicians from these areas went to bat for their constituencies; the Department of Energy responded by increasing their gasoline allotments. These reallocations, however, meant longer lines in other parts of the country.

Complaining of the dramatic increase in the price of diesel fuel, the "double-nickel" speed limit, and inflexible shipping rates, a number of independent truckers took the law into their own hands. Daring the police to move their rigs, they blocked interstate highways and blockaded diesel fuel depots. Truckstops, once relatively pleasant meeting places, became scenes of confrontation among customers and owners. Because of the threat of violence, many truckers refused to go out on the highways; when they did, many went in convoys. Tanker trucks required police escort. The lawless threatened to shut down the country. The government reacted to the media blitz of the truckers with an immediate rate increase.

When farmers paraded around the Capitol and the White House in late winter demanding, among other things, special consideration in the allocation of fuel, President Jimmy Carter guaranteed them sufficient diesel fuel for the summer. In June the president reallocated fuel from the farmers to the truckers. One got the distinct impression that summer that fuel was being allocated according to one general rule: "He who raises the most hell gets the most fuel." Surely the authority of the government to enforce any law encountered a setback during the summer of 1979. Nonetheless, the media, especially television, must have loved it all; the whole show was partially orchestrated for their benefit.

Congress was not about to miss out on the show. Virtually every member expressed heartfelt concern for consumers who had to pay higher prices for gasoline and demanded that a national energy policy be developed. The only problem was that they seemed unable to agree on what that policy should be. Each member seemed to want a "national" policy that favored his or her own district (certainly not one that put his or her own district at a disadvantage). Are domestic oil companies holding back supplies of gasoline? Is the crisis the fault of foreign producers or the president? Are we really running out of energy? Should we inaugurate a crash program for the development of alternate energy sources like solar and wind power? How do we stop energy waste? How do we keep the oil companies from making too much money? These were the types of questions raised that summer from the nightly news to the back porch.

To anyone with the slightest understanding of how the market operates, the energy shortage and the political reaction to it looked like one big circus. It was all so unnecessary. The "man of systems," to use Adam Smith's words, had imagined that he could control and direct the actions of producers and consumers of oil with "as much ease as the hand arranges the different pieces upon the chess-board." He had failed, however, to realize that "in the great chess-board of human society, every single piece has a principle of motion of its own, altogether different from that which the legislature might choose to impress upon it."[2]

In microcosm, the energy debacle of 1979 reflected the triumph and tragedy of a philosophical transition that had been under way in this country for several decades. Until the 1930s or 1940s, individualism was the dominant social philosophy. Under this world view, the individual is free to make decisions affecting his life and is expected to assume full responsibility for the decisions made. Individualism has now been extensively replaced with "collectivism," or "communitarianism" as it has been called. "In the communal model," Harvard business professor George Lodge writes approvingly,

(a) the emphasis is on the organization as a whole, as a community of which the individual becomes a part. As a result, he loses some of his individuality. (b) Authority rests upon a continuing consensus. Considerable effort is spent in developing a sense of participation throughout the organization. It is reported, for example, that the Chinese factory manager performs menial tasks regularly to maintain a sense of community—as if the chairman of the board of GM were to work on the assembly line one day a month. (c) The primary incentive is a strengthening of the nation—for example, building a "better" Japan. And (d) loyalty to the organization is important. Quitting is difficult, if not impossible, and security is high.[3]

In short, we have, to a considerable extent, shifted from emphasizing the moral merit of the individual to stressing the moral worth of the collective—the whole of society. We now make collective decisions on the use of resources and the distribution of incomes. We have elevated the social importance of organization as a structure and have made it an end in itself, denigrating the values possessed by different individuals and suggesting that the public purpose must, in so many new areas, take precedence over the purposes of individuals.

The modern collectivist movement is founded on two assumptions about social organization. First, "social values" have a great deal of meaning and usefulness in guiding public policy. And, second, the organizational structure involving rules, directives, and consensus, that has been used successfully in small groups, like the family, business firms, and clubs, can be applied to the running of the country. Before we move further away from individualism, each of these ideas must be critically evaluated.

THE SOCIAL NONSENSE OF SOCIAL VALUES

Opponents of the free enterprise system are imaginative. On the one hand, they imagine that society is a living, breathing organism, something like themselves, with a mind and will of its own, quite apart from the minds and wills of the people who make up society. This organism has preferences, takes actions based on these preferences, and—unless nurtured carefully—may destroy itself. The advocates of this view frequently use such terms and phrases as "social values," "the public or national interest," "cultural norms," "the collective will," "survival of the culture," "society holds that," and "the will of the people is . . ." They seem to think that social values and norms are often readily discernible and that if not, collective decision-making processes can be devised to discover what they are.

Opponents of the free enterprise system also imagine that society is like a ball of clay that can be pulled on, tugged at, squashed, and molded into some preconceived, desired form by master craftsmen, that is, by social craftsmen who are told, so often in meticulous detail, what these preconceived social values and norms are. The presumption is that if people, acting as individuals, do not achieve the desired social goals, then they can be coaxed or coerced into doing that which they did not do on their own.

This holistic view of society is not completely useless, and nothing that has been said so far is meant to imply that it is. Terms and phrases like "social norms" or "society" are useful in communications because they are abstractions from a complex reality, condensing a number of thoughts into a few letters or words. Further, large groups of people, like nations, can be distinguished from one another by shared values and cultural backgrounds. We know, for instance, that much more than geographical distance separates Americans and Iranians. Indeed, the geographical separation of the two peoples may be the least consequential division between them.

We can all agree on certain general propositions. For example, most of us share a desire for peace and domestic stability. The fighting in Northern Ireland and Lebanon during the 1970s vividly illustrates the suffering that we may have to endure if the rule of law breaks down. We all share an interest in a workable legal system that enables us to resolve conflicts peaceably—that is, in ways that avoid bloodshed and halt the diversion of resources away from productive uses to the destructive and defensive uses of war. Similarly, we all (or practically all) share an interest in bilateral restrictions on nuclear weapons. The accumulation of nuclear weapons for deterrent, if not for offensive, purposes is a potentially deadly game. However, without a recognition of the shared interests of the people involved, the nuclear buildup can become the only game in town. It makes little sense for the superpowers to dig holes in parts of their respective countries to mine the basic metals needed to produce missiles and then to dig other holes in other parts of their respective countries to bury the missiles. Our interests, at least in some respects, are compatible with those of our adversaries. The problem is not one of recognition or denial of these interests; rather, it is one of diplomacy, of finding ways of serving the goals that we share.

Without question, there are a number of social values and cultural norms to which most or all of us readily assent. However, for several reasons we need desperately to appreciate the limitations of the holistic view of society. First, social values are not and cannot be lodged in the "mind of society"; we must be very suspicious of any person who claims ready access to some "truth function" that harbors social values to which all of us should subscribe. Hitler and any number of other dictators have led their nation down the primrose path, claiming they had special cognitive powers for understanding what is and is not good for people as a whole. By definition, social values are held by many different people. One of the most important problems in directing public policy is finding agreement on what values are shared sufficiently to warrant collective or governmental action.

Second, although we may behave as if we always knew very precisely the nature of the social cement that holds us together, we do not. We often intuitively appreciate the basis of our togetherness as people, but we cannot always define it. Words often fail to communicate what we intuitively sense. Written into laws, social values may never acquire the degree of meaning that they have when they are accepted voluntarily by people in their private affairs. The ambiguity of what is left unstated but still implicitly understood can be very important to the continued cohesiveness of groups. Churches have, for instance, gone through considerable internal strain either when the mission of the church was broadened to include, say, political issues or when church leaders have attempted to write down the mission of the church in precise terms. People can be in general agreement that they should "do good," but in substantial disagreement over how the good should be accomplished. In 1979, the Lutheran Church of America decided that it needed a statement of its position on major world problems. Church leaders and members developed what amounted to a political platform for the church. The preliminary version of the platform included the following positions:

> Ours is a world in which wealth is superabundant, exists beside, and depends upon, the poverty and starvation of countless of God's human children. Some humans devour the resources of the earth while innumerable others languish in want and despair. In the cry of the poor is heard the voice of the Righteous One, warning against the continued denial of community through the abuse of recreation.

The platform made several recommendations:

> The church must stand within that struggle, making its voice heard in behalf of the powerless and the forgotten. It must point out that superfluous wealth is an abhorrence to God in a world where, for the majority, economic "failure" means . . . permanent disaster . . . Theological ethics . . . is concerned with the ends to which the productive capacity of a society is put. The church has the divinely-given task of critic and monitor of the economic system . . . The church must be a defender of the rights of the working people, advocating adequate compensation, humane working conditions, and protection against racist and sexist discrimination and abuse . . . As capital becomes increasingly mobile, the church must advance the cause of all persons and communities which may be left destitute

when industry withdraws . . . The church must likewise champion the rights of consumers, advocating public policies which minimize victimization and guard against the marketing of socially harmful products.[4]

The statements are almost platitudes; but as might be expected, many members became upset over the positions taken. Some threatened to leave the church if such political positions were ever officially adopted by the church as a whole; others ignored the debate over the platform, assuming it was just so much political puffery that should not be taken seriously.

A third limitation of the holistic view of society arises from the variety of reasons individuals may have for working together. We may agree to associate with one another and may, as a consequence, give the impression that we agree on why we formed a society, but that does not necessarily mean that we are, in fact, in agreement over *why* we are together. And, there is a significant distinction to be made between voluntarily being together, for purposes that only the individuals understand, and actually being in agreement over what causes us to be together. For example, people often join clubs—small societies—but as individuals they frequently join for different reasons. Some may join a country club because of the sports facilities, others for the chance to meet other people, and some because of the business contacts that can be made. The members may be able to agree on the broad recreational framework of the club within which each is allowed to pursue his or her own interest, but the members may never be able to agree on what each person must do within the framework established. If the club officers start directing in very precise terms what each person is to do in the name of the "identifiable social values" that brought the members together, the result can be considerable dissatisfaction. Coercion may be necessary to keep the members in the club and to get them to do what is supposedly in their common interest.

The same comments can be extended and applied to the formulation of national policy. There is one important difference, however, between the identification of common interests at the club and at the national level. The members of a club voluntarily come together; they choose to be with the other members. Hence, there is considerable likelihood that they are much alike and want many of the same things. At least, there is a greater likelihood of compatibility of interests of people in small voluntary groups than there is among people in states or nations. At the national "club" level, the alternatives open to people are far fewer than they are at the local club level, and the potential for disagreement over unifying values is considerable because of the lack of any significant choice of association. As the size of the group for which social values are defined increases, the potential for differences grows. Further, as the meaningfulness and usefulness of terms like "social values," "cultural norms," and the "will of the people" dissipate, the need for coercion increases and the worth of what is achieved by collective means becomes more and more suspect.

Similarly, as the size of the group expands toward the nation-state, in which people have little choice of association, fewer and fewer issues can acquire the general consent of those governed by the agreement that is reached. To achieve general agreement as group size expands, the issues subject to agreement must become progressively broader and more general. Allowable actions of individuals become less specific, and the wording of agreements struck becomes vaguer and less precise. This suggests that real agreement over what society wants becomes more illusory as we move from organizations the size of a club to organizations the size of a nation. Nebulous wording, which permits the pretense of agreement, can be interpreted differently by different people. As a result, the agreement has little effect on people's behavior, which may be what is desired. Freedom is a very broad social value that garners considerable acceptance among people not only because of its intrinsic value *but* also because it leaves undefined what people can actually do with their lives. It is a framework for individual action—based on individual differences.

When general consensus is sought at the national level, people understandably propose an "effective national energy policy," a "humane health care system," and a "reliable transportation network." In 1946 Congress was concerned that the country would sink into another deep recession, and it was willing to have the federal government assume responsibility for keeping the country off the prewar economic roller coaster of slumps and booms. Few people oppose economic stability or, at least, attempts to avoid another Great Depression. So Congress passed the Employment Act of 1946, which reads in part: "The Congress declares that it is the continuing policy and responsibility of the Federal Government to . . . create and maintain, in a manner calculated to foster and promote free competitive enterprise and the general welfare . . . maximum employment, production, and purchasing power."

Attempts were made to make the act operational by specifying how the government would accomplish these laudable objectives. Agreement on means, however, was not possible. In the 1970s, Congress made another attempt to obtain agreement on national economic planning. The late Senator Hubert Humphrey and Representative Augustus F. Hawkins introduced a bill with specific quantitative inflation and unemployment goals. In 1978 Congress finally passed the Humphrey-Hawkins bill as a memorial to Senator Humphrey, but the final text did little more than restate the employment and inflation goals of the 1946 Employment Act. Adopting a national policy of economic planning without spelling out exactly how the policy will be accomplished is much like agreeing to take a trip without any certain understanding of where the trip will end, how to get to the unspecified destination, and how much the trip will cost. Lack of agreement, however, inevitably emerges when means and costs of achieving the specific objectives in new programs are considered.

THE MAKING OF A POLICY CRISIS

As with all other resources, there is an inherent, inescapable conflict among people for energy. There is simply not enough readily available energy. If there were, energy would be as free as rocks on the barren slopes of the Sierras. Energy has an economic value—it sells for a price—because of its usefulness and because of the limited supply. The price charged for energy is nothing more than the market's means of distributing the available energy among the myriad of competing uses.

Prices serve two important functions in a market economy: they ration the available supply; and they provide buyers and sellers with important information on the relative scarcity of goods and services. If the price of energy goes up, consumers are effectively told that energy has become relatively scarcer compared with other goods and services, and consumers are encouraged to spend their money on other wants that do not cost as much. Further, if the price of energy rises, producers are effectively told that energy, on the margin, has become relatively more valuable to consumers and that they, the producers, should find additional supplies.

This is the way competitive markets work, in general. Markets resolve conflicts, and in the process they weed out the relatively unimportant uses, as indicated by buyers, of energy. Markets do not work perfectly, of course. No one should expect that in an imperfect world. However, they do accomplish extraordinarily complicated problems of transmitting information to buyers and sellers and causing people to adjust to new circumstances.

Beginning in late 1978, Iran, an important exporter of oil, was caught up in an Islamic revolution. Before that, Iran had accounted for about 5 percent of U.S. oil imports, but the revolution resulted in a shortfall in expected supplies. The market could have handled the shortage: the price of gasoline, heating oil, and diesel fuel, as well as of plastics and synthetic fibers, could have risen, reflecting the greater scarcity of oil. Buyers would then have been induced to conserve and look for alternative sources of energy. Producers would have been enticed to look for additional oil supplies and other energy sources. Granted, if prices had risen, so would have oil company profits. Some of their additional income would have been unexpected (even the CIA failed to predict the revolution in Iran). However, some of the additional profit would have been compensation for previous risks the companies had assumed by having reserves on hand to cover an unexpected shortfall in supplies. We had an energy crisis in 1979 for one undeniable reason: the government meddled with the market. The Department of Energy controlled the prices of gasoline and diesel fuel strictly. Certainly, prices did rise somewhat; but price increases were restrained by government pricing formulas. Consequently prices were not used fully as a rationing device, and consumers and producers were denied important information on the true relative scarcity and value of these fuel sources.

The basic conflict over this energy source was present—it will always be present—but the simplest and most efficient way of resolving the conflict was effectively outlawed. The conflict was resolved all right: by congestion at the gasoline pumps, makeshift government allocation decisions, odd-even license plates, restrictions on the number of buying days, and, as we indicated above, by fistfights, gunfire, threats, and hell-raising by those who wanted the attention of the press.

All this was done to avoid a price increase. However, the government was unsuccessful in accomplishing even that objective. Holding the price of gasoline down led to even less gasoline than we could have had in the absence of the price control system. (If nothing else, a higher price would have attracted gasoline away from other countries.) We had less available energy than we could have had, and the restricted supply of energy meant customers were willing to pay a higher price for the restricted quantity. They could not pay the higher price in money, but they did pay a higher "effective price" for gasoline. The higher effective price was simply hidden in the cost of standing in line, the taxes paid for running the Department of Energy, the cost of paying agents to check out the pricing practices of service stations, the inconvenience and lost income due to the inability of people to drive on evenings and weekends, the cost incurred by Congress in its debate on relieving the energy shortage, the reduction in the quality and variety of services performed at service stations, the increased price consumers had to pay for substitutes that were in greater demand because of the restricted supply of energy-related products, the payments due to police and highway patrol departments for their efforts to protect truckers and truck-stop operators, and the higher price paid for farm produce because some crops could not be taken to market. All in all, the price of energy rose above its free-market level; the increase was just disguised—very well disguised.

The energy shortage of 1979 became a crisis, in part, because of the propensity of many well-intentioned people to think of the nation as an amorphous whole for which a national policy, covering a wide range of energy uses, could be formulated. We might all agree that there are instances in which social priorities can be established. For example, in the event of a foreign invasion the military should have priority in the use of fuel over virtually all other users. Similarly, during natural disasters, ambulances should be given priority over people who want to go to stock-car races. These are instances in which broad-based public agreement among individuals defines social values and in which markets may work too slowly. Agreement on some issues, however, does not imply the existence of a well-defined set of social values covering a broad range of other energy uses that can be used to mold a policy in the public's interest. Agreement, which determines the meaning of social values, is simply not present. With these thoughts in mind, we can carefully scrutinize several claims made by advocates of a national energy policy.

During the crisis we heard much talk about the "waste" of gasoline. Many politicians, newscasters, and people on the street were certain that irresponsible people were squandering a lot of energy. Accordingly, President Carter, Secretary of Energy James Schlesinger, and Secretary of Transportation Brock Adams, in particular, made frequent pleas to stop wasting fuel and start conserving the limited reserves we had. The phrase "Don't be fuelish" became popular. Many of the people concerned believed that waste could be meaningfully defined in a social sense, and the emotive connotations of the word "waste" led one to believe this. Indeed, it is difficult for anyone to be opposed to waste; it is like being against responsible behavior.

Popular support for the elimination of waste, however, hides considerable disagreement over what waste is. The rule "One person's waste is another person's need" should not be forgotten in collective efforts to control social waste. Many people use gasoline to joyride; that use seems wasteful to many. But, it is difficult to see why, in the cosmic sense of things, that such a use of energy is any more wasteful than the use of gasoline to go to the beach, or a football game, or any other activity for which the objective is pretty well defined. Cannot some people get just as much value from riding around as others get from going somewhere specific?

President Carter seemed to think in the winter of 1979 that there was some grand ordering of social priorities that would lead any sane person to the conclusion that agriculture should receive top priority in government decisions to allocate fuel. One might agree with such a position, although reluctantly, if the entire nation were on the verge of starvation. However, it is a very difficult decision to justify when so much of the country's farm produce goes into refined foods that have little or no nutritional value, such as candies, condiments, soft drinks, dog and cat food, jellies, pies, cakes, and decorations at fine restaurants. Much food is simply turned into excess weight on a population already millions of tons overweight; much of the food (which was produced with energy) is simply thrown away. Given the variety of circumstances in which people find themselves, who would be so arrogant as to specify the "proper" food purchases of all 225-plus million people in the country? We all may oppose waste, but how can we define waste so that government policies can be made operational? When it comes to the nitty-gritty of policy formulation, can any collective decision-making process handle the burden of defining waste? What happens to freedom when such decisions are made on even a limited basis? It is interesting that Secretary Schlesinger was, during the crisis, referred to as the "energy czar," which tells us much about the social consequences of defining specific social values.

When energy is cheap, we naturally use it for relatively unimportant purposes—as we define relatively unimportant purposes. Why not? At low prices we can afford frivolous uses of energy. By controlling the price of energy, the government simply distorted the signals given consumers. Because the price was being held in check, consumers were led to believe that the relative scarcity of energy had not changed very much. Under those circumstances, why cut back? Why not consume? Why should anyone believe President Carter was leveling with the public about an energy shortage when the price of a gallon of gasoline was cheaper than the price of a gallon of Kool-Aid?

Not unexpectedly, pleas for energy conservation have little impact. Each person can reason that his energy consumption is a minute portion of the country's total. If he uses more relatively cheap energy, no one will know the difference. His energy consumption is too small to count for much. If he cuts back, the same reasoning applies: he will have no significant effect on the long-term energy reserves of the country. The average person is apt to reason that given an energy shortage, any fuel he does not use will be gobbled up by someone else for a purpose that may be no more valuable than his. If energy was wasted in 1979, it was because of the government's attempt to hold the market in check. Governmental actions had the opposite effect of that intended.

In 1979 many people were concerned about rapid depletion of oil, an exhaustible energy source. According to proponents of energy conservation, social values dictate that we should reduce the consumption of any nonrenewable resource. Again, such a social goal achieves considerable support within the voting population, but broad-based support obscures disagreement over how the goal is to be achieved. Which uses should be forgone? How should we choose the uses to be forgone? Collectivists effectively sidestep these critical issues. But until those issues are addressed, loose talk about social priorities make the market appear to be a relatively poor mechanism for allocating resources among competing uses.

During the energy crisis, Congress legislated the 55 mile an hour speed limit on the grounds that it would help preserve our exhaustible gasoline supplies. Did Congress achieve its objective? People who abstained from driving engaged in other activities, using resources that were just as exhaustible as oil. Those who observed the lower speed limit spent more time on the road. Moreover, each hour on the highway is definitely an hour gone forever. The lower speed limit simply reduced the use of one exhaustible resource, gasoline, and increased the use of another, time.

Collectivists tend to look on people's time as inexhaustible because of their proclivity to think of society as a whole (as opposed to a collection of different individuals). The life of "society" is obviously renewable; it can be extended by procreation (which, I might add, can be manipulated by government tax policies); the time lost by those going 55 can be replenished by the birth of other people. If society is the focal point of social policy, lost time is of no concern. Nothing is really given up when energy is conserved by lower speed limits; reduced speed limits, therefore, look like an obvious, albeit partial, solution to a complex problem. If, however, an analysis of society begins by asserting the worth of individuals, a lower speed limit is not an obvious solution at all.

During the energy shortage, a number of people asserted that a small number of producers with substantial monopoly power to restrict industry output and raise prices controlled the gasoline market. Given the thousands of small and big firms in the oil business (no firm controls more than 10 percent of the gasoline business in the United States), such a claim is obviously false.[5] However, the relevant question here is Did government controls on oil production and sales increase or decrease the monopoly power of firms within the oil industry? Clearly, if controls had any effect at all, it was to increase monopoly power. During the crisis, gasoline was allocated to service stations on the basis of the previous year's sales. Because they could not obtain gasoline, new stations could not enter the retail market. Existing stations could cut back on the quality of service without fear of someone else's entering their market and taking away their sales. Furthermore, when supplies were short, refining companies had little incentive to serve stations that were not affiliated with them. Refineries were induced to meet only the minimum requirements of the government allocation system; they did not have to meet the demands of competition in the marketplace because competition was precluded by price controls. The result was long lines at the gas pumps.

During the crisis a number of people contended that available gasoline supplies should be allocated by some nonmarket means like coupons. The presumption, again, was that there is some social function that can tell us how coupons could be allocated "fairly" and "equitably." Such proposals beg critical questions: Do we allocate the coupons by the number of cars people have? What about the family that has five cars, three of which generally sit idle in the driveway? Consider the effects on the demand for junk cars. Do we limit coupons to a maximum of three cars per family? What about the very large family, all of whose members work and need to use their cars? Should we allocate coupons on the basis of the number of licensed drivers? Does that mean every 16-year-old gets the same number of coupons as every 45-year-old? If licenses are used for distributing coupons, will people obtain licenses just to get the coupons? Should the coupons be distributed on the basis of the number of employed workers in a family since people do need gasoline to get to work? Why shouldn't elderly retirees who like to take drives on Sunday afternoon in the country be given coupons? Drives in the country may seem frivolous, but are they any more frivolous than coloring books manufactured by people who drive to work?

If government controls the price of gasoline, a shortage of gasoline will develop, and rationing coupons, no matter what basis is used for distributing them, will command a price in the market. Those willing to pay a higher price for gasoline will gladly buy coupons from those who are unwilling. When the price of coupons is added to the pump price, elementary economics tells us that the overall price will be higher than the free market price. Because they have an economic value, coupons translate into wealth. Holders of coupons are effectively given part ownership to gasoline that they did not produce.[6] Is it any fairer or more equitable for the government to do that than for it to take crops away from farmers and distribute them free to grocery store patrons?

The list of unanswered questions relating to nonmarket means of rationing like coupons is endless. This is because no government bureaucracy is sufficiently talented to define all of the endless differences in personal circumstances, much less fashion its rules to account for all the differences. After considering all the problems that would surface in a coupon system, columnist George Will concluded: "The only rational rationing is price rationing: letting prices rise until supply and demand are in rough balance. But the public flinches from this, and government hates it because it works without government."[7] In summary, all of these claims—the need to eliminate waste, the depletion of nonrenewable resources, the monopoly power of oil suppliers, and the desirability of rationing systems—serve to illustrate one point: when it comes to allocating the nation's resources among competing uses, the concept of social values is largely a social mirage, appealing but inane.

THE TYRANNY OF THE MAJORITY

Stripped of rhetorical camouflage, much contemporary discussion of social values and norms stands naked as an expression of the values of relatively small groups who want the aid of government in their pursuit of their interests. Many people are inclined to support price controls on products like gasoline because they have nothing better to do with their time than stand in line. Many support the closing of gasoline stations on weekends because they either do not plan to go anywhere or can go where they want on weekdays. Many support the 55 mile an hour speed limit because they are not in a hurry. Many propose that gasoline be distributed by coupons because they want to be given, free of charge, an ownership claim to a product for which they did not work.

George Bernard Shaw once wrote that "any government which robs Peter to pay Paul can always depend on the active support of Paul." It is time that we recognize so many of the collectivists for what they are: the Pauls of the world. They tend to think of themselves as anointed with God-given powers to tell the rest of us how to live. They do not mind handing over considerable power to government to pursue the "public good" so long as it is their good that is pursued, but they object to giving the same privileges to people whose values and preferences are at odds with theirs. Thus, they do not regard equality before the law as an important legal, social, and moral principle.

More than a hundred years ago, John Stuart Mill warned that

> the will of the people, moreover, practically means, the will of the most numerous or the most active *part* of the people; the majority, or those who succeed in making themselves accepted as the majority . . . *may* desire to oppress a part of their number; and precautions are as much needed against this, as against any other abuse of power . . . In political speculations "the tyranny of the majority" is now generally included among the evils against which society requires to be on its guard.

Mill concluded:

> There is a limit to the legitimate interference of collective opinion with individual independence; and to find that limit, and maintain it against encroachment, is as indispensable to a good condition of human affairs, as protection against political despotism.[8]

Imbued with a romantic view of democracy, the collectivist imagines that democratic decisions (especially those he favors) are spontaneous social revelations of the collective will. He fails to see collective decisions for what they so often are: the will of those who happen, at the time, to form the majority and who are able, through the democratic form of government, to impose their will on others. He fails to understand that we need constitutional constraints on government as a means of restraining the majorities in society from willy-nilly imposing themselves on the rest of us. He certainly fails to appreciate a fundamental fact: because the market defines the realm of free interaction among people, it is one of those necessary constitutional constraints on government. In this regard, the free market is part of society's internal strategic defense network against coercion.

THE MESSAGE OF FREE ENTERPRISE

Who can forget the first pictures of an earthrise taken from the surface of the moon? Those pictures have profoundly affected our perspective of the place we call home. We know now, with a clarity never before imagined, that we truly do inhabit Spaceship Earth, set adrift in a vast, dark emptiness. Against the barren horizon of the moonscape, Earth looks, despite everything that has happened to it, like the gem of the universe. We are lucky, for from those pictures we can more fully appreciate the accidental nature of our existence, the delicate environmental balance required for our continued existence, and many of the ties that bind us together.

The central message of those pictures is that we share common territories and common interests. The purpose of this chapter has not been to deny that; rather, it has been to argue as forcefully as possible an elemental point: there are limits to the usefulness of the holistic view of society. The sphere that we can see in its entirety from space is not a chessboard, and it is inhabited by individuals who have aspirations and motivations of their own. Certainly, we have common values. Freedom is one of them. Social stability is another. However, when people are given the freedom to pursue their own interests within a "constitution of liberty," they often, as Adam Smith pointed out, serve the interests of society more effectively than if they intentionally try to do so.

Each of us wants to do more than he can possibly accomplish. The same principle applies to society as a whole; there are, perhaps, many more shared social goals than can possibly be achieved. But, government can do only so much; it must be limited *because its abilities are limited*. The problem we face as a country is recognizing that stark fact and using the limited capabilities of government to the best advantage.

When government, for example, is called on to regulate the nation's energy production and consumption (which it need not be asked to do), something must be given up. The energy crisis of 1979 is very instructive because it clearly reveals our propensity to press government to do more than it actually can. The government was asked, during that period, to juggle the demands of competing energy producers and users, and it made a mess of things. The conflict that emerged at the gas pumps between government and farmers, government and truckers, truckers and farmers, and truckers and consumers demonstrated that there is very little agreement (which constitutes the substance of social values) on the allocation of energy. The government should have left the allocation of energy to the marketplace. It should have recognized that by getting involved, it forced people to surrender a little bit of their freedom to buy and sell their goods and services as they wish. Further, it diverted government resources away from treating social issues to dealing with a distribution problem that was being handled with tolerable efficiency by markets. No doubt, more burglaries occurred and fewer crimes were solved during the energy crisis of 1979 because police resources were tied up in escorts for truck convoys. The message of free enterprise is this: let the government concentrate its efforts on the maintenance of a legal framework within which markets can arise; then encourage the government to sit back and let those markets do the job they are designed to do. The government may alter the outcomes of markets, but it should tread softly and carefully and be ever mindful of the trade-offs that it is making.

The
Social Nexus:
Free Enterprise
and the
Constitution

Precepts for living together are not going to be handed down from on high. Men must use their own intelligence in imposing order on chaos, intelligence not in scientific problem-solving but in the more difficult sense of finding and maintaining agreement among themselves. Anarchy is ideal for ideal men; passionate men must be reasonable . . . These are men and women who want to be free but who recognize the inherent limits that social interdependence places on them. Individual liberty cannot be unbounded, but the same forces which make some limits necessary may, if allowed to operate, restrict the range of human freedom far below that which is sustainable.

James Buchanan
The Limits of Liberty

CHAPTER 5

The story is old, but it has much to say to us today. A powerful prince named Fafer ruled the Kingdom of Serendip: "The prince had three male children equally handsome, well made and very promising. As he loved them with extreme tenderness he was willing to have them instructed in all the necessary services to the end that they be worthy to succeed him in his dominions. He called them in one by one for instruction. Then to further their education he sent them out to travel into other lands." In their travels, the three sons made some unanticipated discoveries. They sought one thing, a scroll on which would be found a magic formula for killing the dragons that surrounded the island of Serendip, but they found other, more useful things. They were able to help a caravan leader find a lost camel because of the attention they had paid to the road they traveled and, in the process, made friends with an emperor who had, because of the accuracy with which they were able to describe the lost camel, accused them of camel theft: "They knew he [the camel] was blind in one eye because grass on one side of the road was eaten more than on the other. They knew he was missing some teeth because every step, bits of grass were left untouched. They knew he was lame because one foot dragged on the grass. They knew he carried butter on one side and honey on the other because there were ants on one side which feed on fat and flies on the other which feed on sweets."[1]

Our daily experiences are replete with interesting discoveries made quite by accident—by indirection, by going after one thing and finding another. Indeed, it is not altogether unreasonable to suggest that many of our most valuable findings result from indirection. The late Wallace Hamilton, a noted Methodist minister, filled a career collecting examples of such findings, which he incorporated into his book, *Serendipity*.

He recounts that Columbus discovered America while looking for a shortcut to Asia, that Edison developed the phonograph when he was attempting to invent the light bulb, that puffed rice was discovered when a chemist accidentally dropped a test tube full of rice that had been held over a flame, and that a means of birth control was uncovered by a researcher who was studying sterility. Alexander Fleming's discovery of penicillin; Charles Goodyear's development of the vulcanizing process for rubber; Wilhelm Roentgen's development of the X-ray—all were accidents; all occurred while their inventor was seeking something else.[2] Dr. Hamilton concludes that we often find what we seek and that

> many fine things come out of that [direct] method. We do not minimize its importance, but it has its limitations. It works very well in the material—it's of almost no use in the spiritual. Some of the finest things in life do not come that way. You can get Cadillacs by putting down the cash—not character, not even culture. You can get a house, but not a home. You can get money, but not real riches of life. Some of the most desirable things come by reception, by indirection, from something added and often unexpected in the earnest pursuit of something quite beyond us.[3]

We live in the age of the quick-fix, a time when many are inclined to drown their sorrows in drink or blow their minds with drugs or pop a pill for the slightest ailment. We have a tendency to look for direct solutions to complicated social problems, all too ready to throw more tax money at observed problems in the vain hope that a little more will make them go away. We want directness and we want results. So much of our attitude toward government and its policies is aptly summed up in John Maynard Keynes's quip, "In the long run we will all be dead." We believe government can solve all of our problems if good men and good policies are found, ignoring the effect that a succession of quick-fix policies has on the long-run organization of government.

Part of the reason free markets are mistrusted today is that they do not provide the quick-fix we often seek. The free enterprise system is what it is—a system, an institutional setting that is not designed to conform immediately to every pull and tug of changing social events. The free enterprise system is long-term social policy that must ignore particular circumstances and be judged—in the long run—as a process. The record of the free enterprise system in this country is there for people to marvel at. (Marx was so impressed with the accomplishments of free markets that he believed capitalism was the only system that could develop the industrial base necessary to support utopian communism.[4]) However, that record is not enough for impatient people who demand that something be done today about social ills whose existence is undeniable.

A sustained growth in technology, in industrial production, and in personal income has been the hallmark of economies founded on free market precepts. In retrospect, however, it is difficult to attribute this growth to the free market system. The growth was largely unintended, unplanned; it was largely a serendipity, as assuredly as the discovery of penicillin was. The framers of the Constitution, for example, were after something they valued greatly—personal freedom. They had a plan for freedom over the long run; they got that and something else, an expansion in material welfare. The great mistake of so many present-day reformers is going for the quick-fix. They have a plan for an expansion of welfare. Normally, this means that they are prone to restrict freedom and welfare. Great Britain, the Soviet Union, and New York City are glaring examples of where such directions can lead.

This chapter draws together several strands of thought that surfaced on several occasions in the foregoing pages and tries to give them greater coherence. While recognizing the absolute necessity of government, this chapter also stresses the need to control government by constitutional means, by delimiting what it can and cannot do. Government must be controlled this way partly because of its inherent tendency to grow on its own, but mainly because of the weaknesses of the democratic system as a means of controlling government. Without constitutional constraints on government, a free market system will inevitably destroy itself.

"MINE AND THINE DISTINCT," ONCE AGAIN

Children's play in a sandbox reveals in microcosm much about the larger society of which it is but a speck. The play of children can proceed in an orderly fashion, as if directed and controlled by external forces, so long as the interests of the children do not cross (if, say, each wants to play in separate parts of the sandbox or with different toys). Their play may also be well ordered if the children, having intersecting interests, recognize implicitly or explicitly boundaries for their own behavior, thus acknowledging one another's "rights." When these conditions hold, each child can happily go about the tasks of building sand castles and plotting the imaginary movements of plastic figures; they may also coordinate their efforts by trading services, tools, and toys and build entire communities.

The tranquility in the sandbox can break down—as it often does—when one child fails to recognize the rights of the others and encroaches on their territory. The inevitable result is conflict, harsh words, at first, then a lot of throwing of sand, and finally the destruction of the castles. In such instances, children often look to a third party—a parent. The dispute is normally resolved when the parent gets the children to understand the rules of play and to recognize, once again, the rights of others.

In the larger adult world, our interests are boundless: we want more than we can possibly obtain. We envy others and want much of what they have. In turn, they envy us and want much of what we have. The potential for conflict surrounds our daily existence; and we sometimes teeter, like the children in the sandbox, between order and disorder.

We all desire perfect freedom. We want to be unencumbered by arbitrary restrictions on what we can do with our lives. We want to be free to do what we want, to get what we can get, and to be what we can be. But we can also readily envision what life might be like if everyone enjoyed unlimited freedom. Philosopher Thomas Hobbes believed that without state-imposed restrictions on behavior, we would be in a constant state of war and life would be very unpleasant.[5] Because he was arguing for a strong central state, Hobbes perhaps exaggerated how sordid life could be without a state. On the other hand, we can appreciate an implied point in Hobbes's analysis: complete freedom for all is not possible. We all cannot do all we want to do or be all that we want to be. Our world is much like the sandbox and its abundant potential for conflict. Complete freedom would mean no generally recognized limits to our behavior. Our freedom would, however, be constrained—by the barriers the resulting conflicts would present.

We could solve our problems as children do, by fighting it out, but that would be wasteful. The fights would represent the diversion of resources from productive uses, like farming and construction, to destructive uses, like throwing punches and shaping bigger and better sticks as weapons. Because people would have to eat and sleep, there would be some production. However, many people would devote their time to plundering the production of others or to defending themselves against plundering.

Alternatively, we could resolve our conflicts by defining limits to our own freedom; in other words, we could define the rights that people have. Property is nothing more than a socially recognized list of what people can do with things. When we say we own a particular car, we mean very simply that there are a number of things we can do with that car, but we also mean that there are a number of things we cannot do. Again, the term property defines the boundaries between permissible and impermissible behavior. As UCLA economists Armen Alchian and Harold Demsetz have reasoned,

> In common speech, we frequently speak of someone owning land, that house, or those bonds . . . What are owned are *rights* to *use* resources, including one's body and mind, and these rights are always circumscribed, often by prohibition of certain actions. To "own land" usually means to have the right to till (or not to till) the soil, to mine the soil, to *offer* those rights for sale, etc., but not to have the right to throw soil at a passerby, to use it to change the course of a stream, or to force someone to buy it. What are owned are socially recognized rights of actions.[6]

James Buchanan has noted that "the logical foundation of property lies precisely in the universal need for boundaries between 'mine and thine.' Escape from the world of perpetual Hobbesian conflict requires an explicit definition of the rights of persons to do things."[7] If there were no conflict, there would be no need to define behavioral limits, no need to define property rights. Property gives people latitude to do some things by restricting what all can do: somewhat paradoxically, it provides for freedom by defining limits to behavior.

In an ideal world inhabited by ideal people, that is, by angels, state enforcement of property rights would be unnecessary. Ideal people would acknowledge and fully respect, on their own initiative, the rights of all. However, we live in a less than perfect world, peopled with "passionate men," not angels. We need property to keep people off each other's backs; once property is defined, we need to ensure its boundaries. In short, the state (or some similar collective organization) is needed to define property rights and to protect the rights defined. If rights are not protected by some third-party enforcer, then the rights of each person may be severely restricted: it's back to the jungle.

Recognition of the need for the state, however, obscures an important question about establishing a stable social order: How do we get people to agree on the method of distribution and final settlement of available property? As Buchanan points out in the quotation that heads this chapter, "Precepts for living together are not going to be handed down from on high." Agreement is not always easy to obtain and maintain. Some people feel strongly about what constitutes fairness and equity in the distribution of property; others, because of, say, greater strength, are better off with no agreement on the distribution of property than with property division and state protection of ownership. There are still others who thrive on anarchy and promote it vigorously. To devise any semblance of agreement on the construction of an economic system based on property requires immense intelligence; any settlement is fragile at best. The founders of this country are revered because they worked their way through all of the conflicting views on the type of government and economic system we should have and developed the kind of general agreement so important to the long-term stability of the country. Granted, their task was made easier by the general acceptance by their contemporaries of the notion of private property, but their accomplishments are, nonetheless, remarkable: they got an agreement that lasted for scores of years!

Opponents of the free enterprise system tend to object strenuously to private property and propose, in its stead, state or communal ownership of property. Private ownership, they maintain, gives people too much power; and power corrupts. However, what does state ownership of large chunks of property do to the distribution of power? The opponents of the free enterprise system seem to imagine that the state is some sort of benevolent grandfather who uses his power to serve the ends of his charges. A previous chapter questioned the ability of the state to know what the ends of people are. Here, the question is Why should the state, which is run by mortals, not be disinclined to abuse (and be corrupted by) the power that it has? History is replete with examples of abuse of power by the state—that is, by those who run the state. What happens to freedom—economic and political—when property is concentrated in the hands of those who run the state? Consider the Soviet Union. Again, distribution of property among the people—and away from the state—is a social device for limiting the power of the state. Admittedly, private property is an imperfect means of controlling power—property can be abused by individuals, for example, to influence the actions of the state. Still, the dangers from private ownership must realistically be contrasted with those that can and do emerge when the state usurps the bulk of property and the power that property represents. State control of property, like the presses or pulpits, necessarily implies limitations on individual freedom; it is through the power implied by private property and the resulting variety of options that are subject to choice that freedom has any useful meaning. Property exists, and therefore someone or something must own it. The issue is Which ownership arrangement is best?

To opponents of free enterprise, communal property is the archetype for the fashioning of an entire society. The notion of communal living is attractive on the surface: the idea of people living together in harmony in pursuit of common interests and without the separation among them implied by private property is indeed appealing. Private ownership seems wasteful, inefficient. Many things owned privately are infrequently used. For example, a family's lawn mower is typically used for a couple of hours each week, but only the owner has the right to use it.[8] That does seem like a lot of waste—on the surface, that is. Communal ownership does, in fact, work reasonably well within small groups of people like families, neighborhood groups, and clubs. Families share much in common, a house, the furnishings in it, and the gardens outside. Neighborhoods occasionally hold communal dinners; once the dishes are on the table, no one is prevented from digging in to any of them. Clubs are often formed for the explicit purpose of increasing the use made of such things as tennis courts and pools and thereby reducing the cost incurred by each member.

Communal ownership of property works well within small groups simply because of the small number of people involved. In such groups the activities of any one person are typically a significant part of the sum of all people's activities. This is important for several reasons. First, the attainment of a group's goals often depends critically on each person's doing his portion of the work, or incurring his share of the costs. When one person shirks his duties to the group, both he and the other group members know it; social pressure can be brought to bear on the shirker, ensuring that no one takes advantage of other group members. (A person who agrees to take a dish to a neighborhood potluck dinner will feel uncomfortable arriving empty-handed and without a reasonable excuse.) Second, people in small groups are generally together because they share common interests. They are not forced to associate; they choose to do so and can choose to separate. Their voluntary association usually contributes to an esprit de corps that can play an important function in their collective conduct with regard to their communal property. Third, when a group is small, anyone who abuses the group's communal property can be excluded from the group and thereby denied the benefits of membership. Granted, small groups do not always adhere very well over time and do not always make satisfactory use of their shared property. Nearly half of all marriages can be expected to dissolve in divorce, and many neighbors who join together to buy a lawn mower become enmeshed in disputes over when each owner can use it, how they should use it, and who should be responsible for repairing it. Nonetheless, communal ownership of property by small groups is expected when people are free to make the most of that they have.

It would be nice to be able to conclude that all property in the larger society will be efficiently used when owned communally, with each person able to use all available property at will. However, that is not possible. Many people want to use the same property simultaneously, which cannot be done. Most families own their own lawn mowers because most want to cut their grass on Saturday morning. Besides, relatively inexpensive lawn mowers are available, and the savings from communal ownership of a lawn mower are relatively small. Communal ownership is typically not worth the cost. Where conflicts exist over the use of resources, we must have some means of allocation. Private ownership is one such mechanism. A person who owns property can use it. Anyone who values the property more highly than the owner can arrange to buy the property outright or rent it for a period of time. Without private ownership, we would need some other means of allocating resources among competing uses—for example, first come, first served; random selection; or government fiat. As much economic theory has shown, private ownership and the pricing system are relatively more efficient allocative mechanisms.

Furthermore, in the larger society communally owned property is frequently overused and abused. Everyone has a right to use communally owned property when it is not being used by someone else, and no one has the right to exclude anyone from its use. (Consider the rights people have to public roads, parks, and park benches.) The property is owned by everyone, which is another way of saying that it is effectively owned by no one. No one has to pay directly for its use. Any cost incurred from the use of the property is spread so thinly over the entire population that each individual's use of the property does not materially affect his or her welfare. There are, therefore, few incentives for anyone to care for the property, to restrict its use, or to avoid its abuse. Examples of how communal resources are used and abused in larger society abound.

The lawns on university campuses are communally owned. Generally anyone may walk on the grass. Each walker may kill a few blades; however, each can reason that no one will detect the loss of the grass he has killed. No one will know the difference whether he walks or not. Logic compels *each* individual to take advantage of shortcuts across campus lawns. The usual result is that a path forms on the lawn, marring the beauty of the campus. None of the walkers may want to see dirt paths on campus. Still, it is rational for everyone to keep right on walking; individual actions are inconsequential in the context of the mass. Each person can control only his or her actions, and no one has the right to exclude others from the use of lawns owned communally.[9]

For years most of the airspace and waterways of our country have been communally owned. Everyone has had the right to use them for any purpose without charge, and no one could exclude anyone else from their use. Consequently people have used these scarce resources as dumping grounds for the nation's waste, and many areas have experienced significant pollution problems.[10]

At one time, the grasslands of the western plains were communal property. Anyone could graze his cattle on these ranges. Each cattleman understood that if he did not use the available ranges, then someone else would and that his self-restraint would have no effect on the overall amount of grass. The result was that the ranges were overgrazed and the cattle were underfed. Despite peaceful attempts to control the grazing, range wars broke out among competing cattlemen and between cattlemen and sheepherders.[11]

A number of whale species are near extinction largely because they are being treated as communal property. Whales are for the taking. Anyone can kill a whale free of charge. Although whale hunters may be concerned about the declining whale population, each can reason that if he does not kill the whale he sees, then someone else will and there will be no payoff to his restraint. Since the introduction of new killing techniques and processing ships, whale hunting has become quite efficient; and the consequence of communal ownership has been the wholesale destruction of large populations of whales. In contrast, cattle, which are owned privately, are not close to extinction. Cattlemen have market incentives to control the killing (and breeding) of their herds *because* they are privately owned.[12]

Many people who would never think of throwing their cigarette butts on their front yard readily and without much thought toss them all over public parks, that is, over communal property, creating an environmental mess. Similarly, people who would punish their children for writing on the walls of their own house give the impression that they think the world is waiting to read their immortal words when scrawled all over public restrooms and city buses.

Communal use of property (that is, goods and services) can work well within a larger society when the property itself can be used (or consumed) simultaneously by many different people—when the benefits received by one person from the good do not materially reduce the benefits received by others. In other words, communal ownership works well so long as there are noncompeting uses for the property. National defense is a public good with those characteristics. Everyone within the population benefits from it more or less to the same extent; one person's benefits do not detract from the benefits of others. People are not, therefore, pitted against one another in a struggle for units of the good; there is no problem of allocating the available units among competing uses because the amount of national defense provided does not have to be divided up. All share more or less simultaneously in the defense provided.

The point of this section is that there are strict limitations on the usefulness of communal property ownership as a social device. When people have conflicting or competing interests, property must be divided, "mine and thine" must be distinguished, and boundaries must be drawn for individual behavior. Private property is essential to the efficient organization of society and to the continued existence and enlargement of freedom.

THE DEFICIENCIES OF DEMOCRACY

The failures of the market system are widely recognized and have been, especially since 1960, the subject of much scholarly research. The existence of monopoly power, pollution, and inadequate supplies of public goods and services like schools, parks, and community beautification programs are frequently cited examples of "market failures." The hasty conclusion of many social scientists is that the "government should do something" to remedy virtually all market failures. Even leading economists like Paul Samuelson have fallen into the trap of reasoning that social remedies must be found for problems in private markets.[13]

Although market failures may rightfully be seen as a necessary condition for government intervention in private markets, they are not a sufficient condition. Sufficiency requires that the harm done by observed market failures must be greater than the social costs of governmental efforts to remedy those failures. Often, the cost of government intervention is greater than the potential benefits that can be received; the remedy worsens, not improves, social welfare.

Political economist Gordon Tullock recounts the legend of a Roman emperor who, having been asked to judge a contest between two singers, heard the first singer and immediately awarded the prize to the second singer on the grounds that the second singer could do no worse.[14] This is essentially the approach many social scientists have followed in developing public policy. They have critically evaluated the defects of the "first singer," the market, and have awarded the prize of social control to the "second," the government, without scrutinizing its talents to improve people's lot.

Despite the implied concentration of power in government control of markets, collectivists are unperturbed. They have unflinching faith in the capacity of democracy to restrain government from abusing the power it is given. Collectivists fail to realize that democracy is a highly defective mechanism of control. Other means of control are necessary, as the following examples show.

Single Quantities and Sameness

Democratic decisions are collective decisions made for groups of people. A democratic decision is not necessarily the preferred choice of the individuals involved. Rather, it represents a compromise developed among competing interests. In private markets, individuals can buy what they want at going market prices; they can adjust the quantity to suit their preferences. In democracies, on the other hand, individuals must accept the decision of the majority, adjusting their behavior to the quantity agreed on by the winning majority. An individual may want more fire protection and be willing to bear the necessary extra tax burden but if the majority disagrees at the voting booth, that's tough. He must accept what the majority dictates. Without question, democracies often leave many citizens frustrated, some wanting more, others wanting less, of publicly provided goods and services. Extending the scope of government tends to increase sameness (denying in the process individual differences) and private frustration.

FIGURE 2

POLITICAL COMPETITION IN TWO-PARTY SYSTEMS

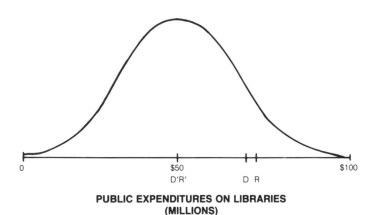

PUBLIC EXPENDITURES ON LIBRARIES
(MILLIONS)

Median Voter Solution

Democratic decisions emerge from a competitive political process. They are not revelations of truth but reflections of the views of voters and the constraints imposed on politicians by competitive politics. Frequently, collective decisions express nothing more than the views and preferences of people in the middle range of the voter distribution. Suppose, for example, that voters are distributed normally along a continuum from $0 spent on public libraries to $100 million. Figure 2 reveals that a few people, represented by the left wing of the distribution, want very little money spent on libraries and a few, represented by the right wing of the distribution, want a great deal spent on libraries. Most people, the hump in the middle of the distribution, would budget a modest amount on libraries, an average $50 million worth.

In a two-party political system the amount of money spent on libraries tends to reflect the views of voters in the middle of the distribution, that is, the median voters. Voters tend to have little choice among candidates for office. Suppose that the Republican candidate takes a political position at R, advocating that $75 million be spent on libraries. By taking that position he can garner some votes. However, if the Democratic candidate takes political position D just to the left of the Republican candidate, advocating slightly less expenditure on librar-ies, he is likely to win the election. The Republican will get the support of all of the voters at or to the right of his own political position, R. (R is closer to these voter's preferred expenditure position than D.) How-ever, the Democrat will get the support of most everyone else.

In order to have a chance of winning the election, the Republican must move to the left of the Democratic, toward the center of distribu-tion. In response, to avoid being defeated at the polls, the Democrat must move further toward the center. The not uncommon result of political competition is for both candidates to be middle-of-the-roaders, taking positions at, say, D' and R' on the continuum and reflecting the preferences of those people in the middle, the median voters. The people in the wings of the distribution consequently have to adjust their behavior to the preferences of those in the middle of the political spectrum.

Many issues must be decided publicly. Although variety in the provision of fire protection is possible, for example, it frequently is impractical. The public must agree on some quantity, and the median-voter solution is probably as good as any. Besides, those dissatisfied with the majority decision can supplement publicly provided fire pro-tection with smoke alarms and sprinkler systems of their own. How-ever, in extending the scope of government through democratic deci-sion processes, we must be cognizant of the nature of the decisions made. It is difficult to see why median voters (or any other group) should be allowed to determine for the rest of the community how much, for example, medical care, retirement income, and playground equipment will be provided. Private markets, to repeat, allow for diversity. Private property prevents one group from imposing its will on the rest; it divides mine from thine.

Political Ignorance

In buying a new car, many people go to considerable trouble attempting to become informed on the merits and defects of various cars. They may read brochures, consult friends on the reputation of local dealers, test-drive a number of makes and models, and even consider professional evaluations reported in publications like *Road and Track* and *Consumer Reports*. They know that their decision will materially affect their future well-being, and this justifies the time devoted to the hunt.

These same people may, however, spend little time investigating the political positions of candidates for public office. They seldom read candidates' position papers or party platforms. They may not even know the candidates' names. They spend precious little time evaluating the soundness of the economic policies espoused by the candidates. They will, more often than not, base their votes on their assessment of each candidate's charisma and character, images derived from television commercials. In short, many people who are quite informed concerning strictly private matters are often quite uninformed—ignorant—about issues in the public forum and about candidates who seek to mold public policy. Still, they may perhaps vote.

These are not ivory-tower speculations; they are unfortunate facts of the political world. In one study, researchers found that the majority of voters did not know which party controlled Congress.[15] A number of years ago, I wanted to assess the impact that basic courses in economics have on the political intelligence of university juniors and seniors in North Carolina. My preliminary survey instrument required the students to name their two U.S. senators and the representative from their home district. I naively thought that practically all university students could readily provide that information. However, 35 percent of the nearly four-hundred students could not give all three names. Ten percent of the students could not remember that one of their U.S. senators was Sam Ervin. This is surprising because the survey was conducted in the middle of the Watergate hearings. (As you may recall, Sam Ervin was chairman of the Senate committee in charge of the investigation and was, during the period, continually quoted in newspapers and nightly newscasts.) When the students were asked to indicate how Jesse Helms, their highly conservative U.S. senator, had voted on major economic legislation, they could do no better than guess.[16] Unfortunately, the study indicated that basic economic courses appear to have no effect on student's political intelligence—their ability to comprehend the political positions of their representatives, their awareness of economic conditions in the country at the time of their representatives' election, or their capacity to understand the consequences of various pieces of important economic legislation.

People are often ill-informed on any matter, public or private. The critical question is Why the disparity in the degree to which people are informed about private matters and public issues? A principle reason is that their individual decisions concerning their individual private affairs affect their personal well-being more directly and decisively than decisions on public issues do. A person knows that a decision on buying a car or a dishwasher can be important to him. On the other hand, he knows that *his* decision on a candidate or public issue will have little or no effect in determining the outcome of an election and, therefore, little or no effect on his future welfare. Certainly, any public decision may affect his future welfare greatly. It may determine his future tax bill. However, the *individual's* decision on an issue has little effect on an election's outcome because in most elections an individual's vote is one among thousands, even millions, of votes. Many individuals reason, quite sanely, that they should not bother incurring the personal cost of becoming informed about public issues and candidates. So they remain largely ignorant about the critical issues of our times.[17] Still, these people are the grass roots, the ones who are supposed to control and direct government's pursuit of the public interest.

This analysis of voter motivation does not imply that all people are completely uninformed about all issues. Obviously, many voters know a great deal about political issues and candidates. There are, however, rational limits to the corporate intelligence of the body politic. People can be expected to understand the broad issues that transcend individual circumstance. However, a political process cluttered with many different issues can confuse voters. With little incentive to do otherwise, they will remain uninformed about most issues. In other words, the intelligence of the voting population that is supposed to guide government can disintegrate as government expands its scope of activities. Government must remain relatively limited and uncomplicated if democracy is to be a controlling force intelligently utilized.

Special Interest Groups

Although people may be relatively uninformed about political issues in general, they usually know a great deal about candidates' stands on issues that affect them directly. For instance, textile workers in South Carolina know that tariffs on textile imports can dramatically affect their job security and wages and are, understandably, alert to candidates' positions on the issue of textile tariffs. They may know little about politics, but they tend to know that. Social security recipients in Florida are often well informed about politicians' positions on social security benefits. Defense contractors keep their employees informed about the defense budget. Supporters of the "right to life" movement zero in on a candidate's stand on abortion. Government workers keep close tabs on what politicians say about government salaries. Indeed, because of its concentrated political interest, each group can be expected to contribute its time and money to candidates whose programs reflect its narrowly focused views. Each may ignore candidates' positions on a broad range of other issues of no direct, personal interest to them. Consequently, a presidential candidate can favor expanded social security benefits in St. Petersburg, Florida; higher tariffs on imported textiles in Greenville, South Carolina; and greater defense expenditures in Seattle, Washington. Obviously, presidential candidates take advantage of the selective ignorance of voters: their many-forked tongues create the coalition of interest groups needed to win an election. The only real problem is the outcome: the potpourri of campaign promises translates into a bloated government budget, something for everyone but too much for the nation as a whole.

In a democracy, special interest groups tend to have political clout disproportionately greater than their numbers would suggest for two reasons: (1) most voters are relatively uninformed about what politicians do for special interest groups; and (2) special interest groups benefit substantially from government programs. Such groups can use a portion of the benefits to make political payoffs and campaign contributions to politicians supporting their causes. The arrangement is cozy: "You pat my back and I'll pat yours." The general public, however, gets robbed in the process.

Voting Inconsistencies

Individuals are able to define, within limits, what they want and, for the most part, can act consistently on their subjective ordering of desires. For example, the choices of an individual ranking goods *A*, *B*, and *C* from most preferred to least preferred in that order are fairly predictable: *A* over *B* and *C*, *B* over *C*. Such preferences are said to be "transitive."

Within a political community the preferences of individuals may be perfectly transitive; each individual may consistently rank and choose among all political options. However, there is no guarantee that the collective decisions of the community will be transitive. Indeed, as Nobel laureate Kenneth Arrow has demonstrated, some pretty screwy results can emerge from politics.[18] Suppose that a political group consists of three individuals, I, II, and III, who rank policy options *A*, *B*, and *C* as follows:

	Individuals		
Ranking	I	II	III
Most Preferred	A	B	C
	B	C	A
Least Preferred	C	A	B

If the group chooses between policies *A* and *B*, then policy *A* wins with the votes of I and III, a majority. If between *B* and *C*, then *B* wins, receiving the votes of I and II. If the choice is between *A* and *C*, however, *C* wins with the votes of II and III. The collective decisions are intransitive: *A* is preferred to *B*; *B* to *C*; and, despite the fact that *A* should be preferred to *C*, *C* wins over *A*.

Although the possibility of inconsistent collective decisions decreases as the number of people and issues increases,[19] we should not be surprised at the occasionally unintelligible decisions of Congress, state legislatures, and voters. Voters have little incentive to determine the options; politicians spend over 60 percent of their time trying to get (re-)elected and little time making sure they understand *and can order consistently* the policy options on which they must make decisions.

Political Expediency

People adhere to principles in personal affairs because of an implied moral duty and the understanding that their ethical code will serve them well over a sequence of decisions. Its violation may, at times, be expedient; they may, however, resist temptation because they do not want to worry over individual problems and believe that in the long run they will be better off standing firm on their principles. For instance, people commonly hold to the principle that they should not steal, not because stealing is never beneficial—most people experience the opportunity of taking valuable property without getting caught—but because they do not want to be continually confronted with deciding whether to steal, because they think stealing is morally wrong, and because they can maintain their freedom from incarceration.

Like the rest of us, politicians may have some strongly held guiding principles for their personal and professional lives. However, in a democracy that is unconstrained by constitutional precepts, even politicians have a problem. Their terms in office last for, at most, six years. And before they can do anything for themselves, their constituencies, or their country, they must be elected and, once in office, re-elected. The pressure of electoral competition may force them to set aside, for the moment, their principles. They may know, in principle, the best policy course for the country in the long run; however, the long run means nothing to them unless they are successful in the short run, that is, in the recurring elections.

For example, in order to solve the problem of simultaneous inflation and unemployment, the policy course of the country should, perhaps, be a gradual and long-term slowdown in the rate of growth of the money stock. (That is the recommendation of a group of economists led by Milton Friedman called "monetarists.") If the money stock were reduced, say, from a growth rate of 12 to 2 percent, within a matter of months the result might be economic havoc. Because prices could not be raised to compensate for double-digit increases in wages stipulated in previously agreed to contracts, many workers would be thrown out of work. Because of the number of workers on the market more or less at the same time, all would have a difficult time regaining employment. On the other hand, if the money supply were gradually reduced from 12 to 2 percent over a period of, say, seven to eight years, worker contracts could be gradually adjusted to account for the slower rise in prices. Some workers would be unemployed, but they would not all be on the market simultaneously. The adjustment to a lower rate of inflation could be relatively smooth.

Why not follow this sane, commonsense policy course? In the short run, within the seven- to eight-year period, unemployment would, perhaps, be a little higher than usual and growth in production and real income would be slower than usual. Again, politicians have to be elected in the short run, and the short-run problems created by the gradual decrease in the growth rate of the money stock would reduce the re-election chances of the encumbents. Having little incentive to comprehend the complexities of and need for a policy course of gradualism, the electorate tends to favor politicians who promise to solve their short-run problems.[20] Consequently, the country stumbles and bumbles, as it has, from election to election guided by short-run quick-fix policies totally inappropriate to the long-term policy needs of the country. Indeed, the quick-fix policy route can lead (and has led) to ever-increasing rates of inflation with no improvement in unemployment.

Consider the history of the U.S. economy since the Kennedy administration. John Kennedy came into office in 1961 on the slogan that he would get the economy moving again. He was convinced that the federal government should attempt to fine-tune the economy, which then had an unemployment rate of about 4–5 percent and an inflation rate of about 2–3 percent. In succeeding elections politicians have had to compete for votes on the basis of pledges to cure unemployment problems immediately. Virtually all have sought short-term remedies for the existing unemployment problem. The result was a gradual rise in the inflation rate to over 12 percent at the start of 1981. The primrose path was there for the taking, and we took it—blindly.

Bureaucratic Control

In a democracy, voters are supposed to control the politicians and politicians the bureaucrats. However, the system does not always work that way. Voters have only limited and intermittent control of politicians. Further, politicians seem at times totally unable to control the bureaucracies they have created. Almost every president in modern history has complained about his inability to get the bureaucracy to respond to his orders. Moving bureaucrats, they complain, is much like pushing on a string that has been cut several times. As columnist Jack Anderson quipped, "Presidents come and presidents go, reaping the calumny, but the bureaucrats endure. These soldiers of the swivel chair remain nameless and unnoticed."[21] But, we might add, as growth in government budgets and scope of activities increases, these soldiers of the swivel chair gain an increasing amount of power, political and economic. They are able not only to allocate with greater discretion the moneys appropriated for their programs, but also to usurp much of the legislative authority of the government. They prepare most of the bills that Congress debates, and in that way, which carries subtle but important powers, they mold the policy course of the country. In addition, under a large government, politicians cannot produce all of the necessary laws; they do not have the time or the inclination to do the required work. Consequently, broad legislative authority is often delegated to bureaucracies, which then write volumes of rules and regulations that are supposed to fulfill the legislative mandate. The writers of these rules are a grand, invisible legislature that is to a considerable extent not controlled by anyone. Politicians have little time and incentive to devote even to understanding what bureaucrats are doing, much less to controlling them. Individual voters lack a motivation for moving the political system to do anything about the uncontrolled bureaucracies. The result is that democracy tends to lose its grip on what government does.

THE CONSTITUTION OF FREEDOM

If people are to be free, then government is necessary. That is the central, unavoidable lesson of the anarchistic jungle in which people can take what they want at will from others. Boundaries on individual behavior free people from the coercion of others. Realistically speaking, government must draw and enforce those boundaries. However, history teaches that people cannot be content to establish government and to turn over to it undefined power to do good. The same people whom government must constrain will surely want to use the undefined or ill-defined powers of government to pursue their own interests. An unconstrained government would bring a return to the jungle and a struggle over boundaries as surely as if government were dissolved.

Government is necessary, but it must be controlled. How to marshal the necessary control, without choking the flexibility needed in a changing world, is one of the most perplexing issues facing contemporary society. Democratic controls on government are useful and necessary; but as I have attempted to show, they are highly defective. As James Madison pointed out, we must take "auxiliary precautions" to prevent government from being abused, to make sure that government is guided by long-term principles of social organization. A constitution for government is a social means of controlling government, for it delimits what government can and cannot do. A constitution can define very broad powers for government, but broad powers may mean that there is little that government cannot do, implying that there is little that people (businessmen and social reformers alike) cannot do through the use of government powers. Again, breadth in the powers of government can lead either to dictatorial rule by a few or to a scramble for the use of government's broad powers by various individuals and interest groups. The consequence could be a form of organized constitutional anarchy in which people are pitted against one another in a struggle over the use of the government's power.

A "constitution of freedom," on the other hand, seeks to minimize conflict and coercion in any form, public or private, by establishing a government and then by restricting, as much as possible, its powers to control and direct people's behavior. Such restrictions can be developed in several ways, and the purpose here is only to develop the broad outlines. In general, a constitution can legitimize the concept of property, handing almost all existing property over to individuals (thus distributing power) and strictly limiting the ability of the government to usurp—through expropriation, regulation, or taxation—private property rights. In addition, as is done by the Bill of Rights, a constitution can explicitly prohibit government intervention into certain areas of human affairs. In short, the constitution of freedom must limit as strictly as possible the types of social issues that can be settled by collective decision-making processes.

Of course, perfect freedom is not possible. Neither is perfect control of government by constitutional means. As a social document, a constitution must ultimately be carved in words that are woefully inadequate to express people's aspirations. A constitution, especially through time, will continually be subject to reinterpretation and, on occasion, misinterpretation. Perhaps, in the final analysis the strength of a constitution will lie not so much in the words that are written as in the value that people place on freedom as a basic value. To maintain a free society, those who value freedom may have to be "eternally vigilant," to continually show, to use Hayek's words, "that liberty is not merely one particular value but that it is the source and condition of most moral values. What a free society offers to the individual is much more than what he would be able to do if *only he* were free" (emphasis added).[22] Frank Knight also saw the problem to which Hayek alluded:

> And the main, serious problem of social order and progress is . . . the problem of having the rules obeyed, or preventing cheating. As far as I can see there is no intellectual solution of that problem. No social machinery of "sanctions" will keep the game from breaking up in a quarrel, or a fight (the game of being a society can rarely just dissolve!) unless the participants have an irrational preference to having it go on even when they seem individually to get the worse of it. Or else the society must be maintained by force, from without—for a dictator is not a member of the society he rules— and then it is questionable whether it can be called a society in the moral sense.[23]

THE SELF-DESTRUCTION OF FREE ENTERPRISE

A constitution forms the boundaries of a free society within which free enterprise will necessarily emerge. People with the freedom implied by private property will, in following their own interests, produce, seek out mutually beneficial trades, and, in general, enjoy the fruits of freedom. The order that emerges will be spontaneous (or self-generating) because though bounded by laws, it will be undirected. The complexity of the system that does emerge will be far greater than could have been imagined by any mind or group of minds.

The free market system is predicated on a restricted government. In investing for the future, people assume considerable risks concerning the course of events. They willingly take risks because of the profit reward that free markets offer. They understand that government, constrained by constitutional precepts, protects their investment. If entrepreneurs feel their investment is unprotected and are uncertain about government intervention in the market—that anyone can take all or a significant portion of the benefits accruing from their investment— they will be far less inclined to take market risks.

No game—parlor or real world—can be well played if the rules constantly fluctuate. The greater the flux, the greater the uncertainty in playing the game. In short, when constitutional, long-term guiding precepts constrain what government can do, investors do not have to worry that government will, suddenly and without warning, change the rules of property and use its power to take away, at some future time, either their investment or the income that they expect. An unrestricted government can bob about in the development of its economic and political policies, increasing risks entrepreneurs face and reducing their inclination to do what they are supposed to do—produce, trade, and, in general, enjoy the fruits of freedom.

In modern times, most of the world's governments, including that of the United States, have largely shaken loose from constitutional restrictions. They have assumed in the process ever-larger roles in directing social and economic activity. (Chapter 2 recounts the proliferation of new national policy courses.) The result of uncorked government has been that people are no longer certain of what government *cannot* do, no longer sure of what government will do next. This uncertainty has led to a loss of individual freedom, an increase in the instability of the social and economic system, a reduction in business investment and creative activity, and a general disillusionment with free enterprise as a viable economic system. Many people fail to see, however, that it is not the free market system as a system that is responsible for many of our social and economic troubles, but that the withdrawal of a firm *constitutional* foundation for government has undermined the free enterprise system. This is causing the free market system to falter, for no economic system can remain stable if the underlying political system is unstable.

If government is constitutionally unrestricted, free enterprise will destroy itself. Entrepreneurs, interested in making a buck, will use their talents to manipulate democratic governments to pursue their ends, thus expanding the bounds of government even further. As noted earlier, entrepreneurs will be caught in a competitive struggle for special government favors. Under an unrestricted government, textile firms will seek tariffs on imported textiles; steel producers will seek special quotas on steel imports; defense contractors will lobby for an expanded defense budget; colleges and universities and their suppliers will push for increased government funding of public and private education; automobile producers will seek special grants to develop futuristic, energy-efficient automobiles; publishers will lobby for special postal rates to ship books and magazines; farmers will work for higher price supports for their crops; truckers will seek protection from competition through regulation by the Interstate Commerce Commission; home builders will promote tax advantages for homeownership;

banks will seek government controls restricting interest rates on deposits; the list could go on and on.

Each move that a business (or any other) group makes to secure special government favors will mean another bit of freedom erased for someone somewhere. Like the student who contemplates taking a short-cut across the campus lawn, however, each business group reasons that granting its particular request matters little in the context of the whole. By stressing some noble social purpose served by its product (almost all goods serve some beneficial social purpose), each group justifies the favor it receives from government. When government is unrestrained, the logic of using government whenever and wherever possible is compelling to interest groups. The problem is, however, that the government fast becomes a social cesspool, making everyone (or practically everyone) worse off as people divert their energies away from productive market uses to unproductive political uses and abuses. As the nineteenth-century French economist and social satirist Frédéric Bastiat pointed out, government can become that great fiction in which everyone believes that he can live at the expense of everyone else. An unconstrained government can lead us back to the jungle as surely as constrained government led us out of it. In Hobbes's governmentless jungle, people fight with fists and clubs; in the modern jungle with government, the weapons used are more refined and the blows less direct and visible. The result is the same in both jungles: people are deprived of freedom. Adam Smith's classic work indicates the true spirit of the free market system:

> The proposal of any new law or regulation of commerce which comes from this order of entrepreneurs, ought always to be listened to with great precaution, and ought never be adopted till after having been long and carefully examined . . . with the most suspicious attention. It comes from an order of men, whose interest is never exactly the same with that of the public, who have generally an interest to deceive and even to oppress the public and who accordingly have, upon occasions, both deceived and oppressed it [through public and private means].[24]

BUSINESSMEN AND FREE ENTERPRISE

In the quest for social justice, collectivists have seriously weakened, if not destroyed, the constitutional boundaries of government. They have failed to realize that social justice must ultimately emerge as a serendipity from the search for a more fundamental value, individual freedom. Seeing weakened boundaries of government and profitable opportunities in redistributing national income, private entrepreneurs, representing both social and business groups, have sought to pursue their own interests through government. This is the central theme of this book.

One final question needs to be addressed: Do businessmen and women really want free enterprise? On the surface, the question seems silly. Of course they do—or, at least, that is what they profess. However, the question is not trivial because large segments of the population are now disgruntled with what they observe happening in government and through government action. Many people espouse a return to free enterprise principles. What seems contradictory, however, is that many supporters of free enterprise are as eager as everyone else to use government to their own advantage. For example, Thomas Murphy, chairman of the board of General Motors, in a widely distributed advertisement, came out in full support of President Carter's 1979 "voluntary" wage and price guidelines. One must wonder if GM's fear of losing government contracts partially motivated its chairman's stand.[25] Charles Koch, chairman of Koch Industries and the Council for a Competitive Economy, gives several examples of business support of government intervention:

> A. E. Benning, chairman of Amalgamated Sugar, insists that "if relief from the world market price levels is not provided by government, much, if not all, of the domestic sugar producing industry will disappear."
>
> William T. Cassels, Jr., president of Southeastern Freight Lines, opposes deregulation of the trucking industry. It would, he asserts, "create havoc in the present transportation network, to the detriment of the American public."
>
> Thornton Bradshaw, president of Atlantic Richfield, tells us in his *Fortune* magazine article ominously titled, "My Case for National Planning," that key decisions on energy production "can only be made at the highest level of government, with the imprimatur of the president."[26]

Koch continues with the question, "What's going on here? Have America's business leaders gone mad? Why are they cutting their own throats—by voluntarily and systematically delivering themselves and their companies into the hands of government regulators?"[27] Without doubt, many people have asked the same question. Some people have understandably lost confidence in the free market system and have concluded that the American economic system is one of welfare and government protection for the wealthy and free enterprise for the poor. The impression is not entirely wrong. However, the contradiction between what people say and what they do (presented in Chapter 1) is to be expected when government is not contained by the rule of a constitution that rises above circumstances and the people who happen, at any moment, to govern.

Controls on government are a means of controlling and of constraining business, or any other social group, from imposing its will on the rest of us. Businessmen, as a group, are like anyone else. That is to say, many of them would like to expand their freedom at the expense of others. They do not want to compete—to have to outdo, outproduce, and underprice other producers. They want to control their markets. They would like to use the powers of government to further their own ends. They prefer a world in which government uses its powers differentially to enhance their company's profits and market position. After all, they, like the rest of us, want higher incomes and think that their activities are ultimately for the good of society. However, many businessmen understand that when government is able to help them by differential use and abuse of its powers, it is also free to help a host of other firms and industries. And the sum total of all government intervention must necessarily be detrimental to all firms in all industries.

For example, dairymen readily encourage the government to support the price of milk and to buy the resulting surplus at artificially high prices. Such differential uses of government power increases the incomes of dairymen. However, similar use of government power in the trucking industry, while helping truck owners, harms dairymen: dairymen must pay more to have their products delivered to market and, because of the higher transportation costs, must pay higher prices for all the goods they, as consumers, buy. If government treated all industries the way it treats milk producers now, virtually everyone would be worse off—their incomes would be lower—because market restrictions, on balance, increase production costs and reduce the nation's output.

In short, businessmen can be expected to favor the extension of government powers so long as it improves their welfare. In the final analysis, however, they must prefer controls on government—a system of free enterprise—to a system in which everyone has access to and uses government's redistributive and coercive powers. The case for free enterprise makes sense to businessmen only so long as we adhere to a fundamental legal principle: equal treatment under the law. Under that rule, businessmen can readily envision the disastrous state that would result if everyone had equal access to government power and was accorded government favors.

When government is unconstrained, businessmen are forced to compete for the use of government powers. They know that those who secure the use of government powers flourish and those who do not perish. Under an open-ended government, businessmen are caught on the horns of a true social dilemma: they are damned if they do enlist government aid and damned if they don't. They can be called hypocrites for espousing free enterprise and, at the same time, seeking government aid. They can also appreciate that government intervention contributes to the slow demise of the free enterprise system. Yet, if they do not enlist the aid of government, their competitive market position can be eroded by others who are subsidized and protected by government.

Businessmen realize that their stockholders want them to earn the greatest profits possible. If money is to be made or losses prevented by appeals to government, then executives must make those appeals or jeopardize their position. Chrysler President Lee Iacocca went to government with his hands cupped because it was a way of transferring the risks and losses of doing business from his company and stockholders to the rest of the population. However, he could not have avoided the trek to Washington even if he had felt it was wrong. If he had not sought the bailout, he would have been replaced.

When government is unbounded, businessmen must become public beggars. When the powers of government are strictly limited, then the energies of executives can be directed at doing what they do best: expanding production, controlling costs, and increasing profits. Iacocca realizes that in the case of the Chrysler bailout he and his company gained by government intervention. But he must surely realize that if every other company in a similar financial position is treated the way Chrysler has been, then he, his company's employees, and most everyone else will be the worse off. Government bailouts take away the incentives people have to avoid losses; hence, more losses and more bailouts can be expected. Businessmen must need and want free enterprise because it is a system that protects them from themselves. We all need the same protection; the old adage that power corrupts applies to all groups who, like businessmen, have an identifiable interest that can be aided and abetted by government.

In answer to the question, "Have America's leaders gone mad?" Charles Koch expresses a measure of hope for the future:

> The answer, of course, is simple. No, business executives do not share a collective death wish. They *think* they're gaining special advantages for their firms by approving and encouraging government intervention in the economy.
>
> But they are deluding themselves. They are selling out their futures for a few short-run benefits. In the long-run, by helping to make government powerful enough to destroy them, they will suffer the consequences of their blindness. And they'll deserve everything they get.
>
> Fortunately, not all business people are so shortsighted. *A substantial number want nothing more from government than to be left alone.*[28]

Perhaps businessmen will follow their present course to social suicide, to the death of the free market system that they have nurtured and which has nurtured them. Perhaps Koch and others are much too kind to businessmen. On the other hand, They may indeed see the folly of the present system of virtually open-ended government. Ultimately, free markets and constitutional government go hand in hand. Businessmen must comprehend this transcending social nexus. Otherwise, we will surely continue our gallop down the "road to serfdom."[29]

"The Governmental Habit"

All in all, we work from January 1 to nearly the end of April to furnish the wherewithall for government spending; only then can we turn to providing for our private needs . . . This situation would be dangerous to our liberty even if we were getting our money's worth from present government spending. But there is scarce a man so rash as to say that we are.

Milton Friedman
An Economist's Protest

CHAPTER 6

Professor Friedman wrote these words in 1967. The message is as important today as it was then, perhaps more so: "tax independence day" is now observed in late May. Despite all the complaints, government marches relentlessly into new areas. Chapter 2 notes that growth in government regulation of the economy has been as impressive as growth in total budget expenditures. Explaining governmental growth has been a major concern of economists. Economic historian Johathan Hughes attributes it simply to a "governmental habit," an innate propensity of government to expand based on nothing more than the bedrock of past policies.[1]

Each expansion of government superficially appears quite logical, even reasonable, when considered by itself. However, a series of small sorties enlarging the perimeter can understandably cause concern over the direction of the line of march. Can we actually be sure that governmental growth will stop short of extensive, if not complete, control of our economic lives? The question is important because government appears to be out of control and people are bewildered by its inability to act and to solve problems.

This chapter does not provide a complete explanation for governmental growth—if only we could do that. It does continue with the theme that growth in the public sector is due, in part, to undue reliance on majority-rule government unchecked by constitutional constraints. This chapter is expressly concerned with the effect of the "power of ideas" on governmental growth. More specifically, it deals with the impact of Keynesian economics and the theory of market failure on the development of public policy through political means. Its obvious concern is the use of economic justifications for governmental actions, which have been developed and refined in the twentieth century, to extend government to a size and scope far beyond initially planned limits. In addition, however, it deals with the resistance of the political system to a return to limited government. Two central questions are addressed: How can the economic argument for limited government be converted, by political means, into an argument for self-perpetuating government growth? And, if so many people are concerned about the present size and scope of government, why does the political system resist, stubbornly, reductions in the public sector and embrace, enthusiastically, further extensions of government?

THE CONSEQUENCES OF LORD KEYNES

John Maynard Keynes, the British economist who developed the basic theory for much modern "macroeconomic policy," once wrote,

> the ideas of economists and political philosophers, both when they are right and when they are wrong, are more powerful than is commonly understood. Indeed, the world is ruled by little else. Practical men, who believe themselves to be quite exempt from any intellectual influences, are usually the slaves of some defunct economist. Madmen in authority, who hear voices in the air, are distilling their frenzy from some academic scribbler of a few years back. I am sure that the power of vested interests is vastly exaggerated compared with the gradual encroachment of ideas.[2]

As Keynes fully appreciated, ideas do play an important role in directing public policy. Little did he realize, however, that he was writing his own epitaph.

In times of heavy unemployment, like the 1930s, Keynes argued for a then radical policy course. He proposed that government should spend more than it collects; that it should purposefully run a budgetary deficit. When government spends more than it takes out of the economy in the form of consumer spending power, it increases, so the argument goes, total demand in the economy.[3] In this way government stimulates private production of goods and services and hence reduces unemployment. Indeed, Keynes contended that an increase in government spending without a compensatory increase in taxes could conceivably increase national income by two or three times as much—that is, government fiscal (tax and spending) policy could have a significant "multiplying" effect on the economy. According to Keynesian theory, which has been refined and extended by other economists, the debt accumulated through government's efforts to remedy unemployment is no problem. In fact, it is on balance beneficial because the debt results in greater output of goods and services (effectively "free" since nothing is given up) and in improved efficiency in the private sector of the economy since resources are more fully utilized.

Economists James Buchanan and Richard Wagner have argued that the widespread acceptance of Keynesian economics is a major cause of much modern governmental growth.[4] They contend that before the Kennedy administration's explicit acceptance of Keynesian policy recommendations in 1960, Congress was constrained in what it could do by the need to match expenditures with tax receipts—by what Buchanan and Wagner call the "balanced budget norm." Politicians in the pre-Kennedy era, before the adoption of Keynesian economics, did increase expenditures and sometimes incurred budget deficits, but the public and the press tended to call on them to justify their actions and politicians tended to apoligize for their "fiscal irresponsibility." Now, with the balanced budget norm effectively broken and with the full blessing of most professors and journalists, government is less concerned about its spending proclivities. Keynesian analysis has been largely repudiated by experience; however, it continues to provide politicians interested in election and re-election the economic justification (or excuse) they need to spend more than government collects in taxes. It has given politicians a chance to offer their constituencies more government programs, goods, and services than they are asked to pay for through taxes.

Through the effect that government deficits have had on the Federal Reserve's inclination to expand the money supply, they have contributed to inflation. The public always pays for expanded government programs, but the true costs are obscured by price increases that seem only remotely connected to these programs. As Chapter 5 argued, many voters have little incentive to associate deficit spending with inflation; they can more easily see the benefits of government building projects delivered to their districts by their congressmen. Deficits result from an elaborate and tedious political process, making it possible for politicians to absolve themselves of responsibility by blaming each other. Further, private firms usually receive much of the blame for inflation since they are the ones that actually raise prices.[5] Politicians could not have dreamed up a more tempting economic platform! The seductions of the argument have evidently been irresistible, for during the 1960–1980 period, the federal government incurred a significant budget deficit in every year but one. The total debt during the period reached $717 billion, more than two and a half times the total accumulated by the federal government in all years before 1960.

Ideas have consequences! Keynes recognized that elementary point, but he failed to appreciate fully the political consequences of his own ideas. He did not imagine that the policy recommendations enshrouded in his esoteric theories would one day be the blueprint for guiding the economies of most developed countries. What economist could harbor such a vain hope. As Keynes's biographer Sir Roy Harrod has noted, he had an elitist world view. Keynes seemed to imagine that public policy would be worked out by an "intellectual aristocracy using the methods of persuasion," not by ordinary men and women with political aspirations who are willing to bend policy recommendations, good or bad, to suit their own political objectives. Politics is a grubby business and must be recognized as such by theoreticians in their ivory towers. This is another reason why democracy as an institutional art form must be constrained by, to repeat Madison's words, "auxiliary precautions." Before Keynes, we had the balanced budget norm, which though unwritten was nonetheless binding; now, we must look for substitutes. That is the cause behind the Proposition 13s of the country.

THE ECONOMIC JUSTIFICATION
FOR GOVERNMENT

The purpose of any theory is to focus attention on a restricted set of causal relationships and to foster, within bounds, an intellectual myopia. In the social sciences in particular, a researcher cannot possibly consider all social relationships observed in the real world and, at the same time, make sense of them. To make his task manageable, he must narrow his field of vision. This approach enables him to hone in on specific problems and to recommend policy solutions. The process, however, leaves many secondary effects of policy unconsidered, either because they are of no direct concern to the researcher or because they are deemed inconsequential. In the case of Keynesian economics, the attempts of policymakers to fine-tune the economy were undeterred by the inherent political problems, which Keynesianism simply ignored.

Government intervention in the private sector of the economy is also justified on grounds of efficiency. (Preceding chapters have considered this explanation briefly.) Most goods benefit exclusively the person who owns them or consumes them. Candy bars, watches, clothes dryers, and houseplants tend to benefit only their owners; no one else is affected by their production or purchase and use. The market can produce and distribute such goods efficiently. Those who benefit from the goods can buy them. Those who produce the goods can withhold them and deny potential buyers their benefits unless payment is made. Production of the good can be expanded so long as buyers are willing to pay producers at least as much as the good costs to produce.

However, some goods have "spillover effects," sometimes called "external costs and benefits" or just "externalities," meaning that their production or consumption affects people other than owners either negatively or positively. A lighthouse is an example of a good with spillover (external) benefits. People other than the owner profit from the warning light; passing boats cannot be denied the benefits of the lighthouse. Because the benefits cannot be withheld until payment is made, it is difficult to imagine private entrepreneurs producing lighthouses as a profit-making venture on a free market. Like national defense and police protection, lighthouses tend to be provided publicly, if they are provided at all. Hence, the economic literature refers to goods with external benefits as "public goods" (when the community at large receives most of the benefits) or "quasi-public goods" (when owners and the larger community share the benefits). A retail merchant who improves the appearance of his storefront provides a quasi-public good. He benefits because more customers are attracted to his store; people in the community benefit by having a more attractive shopping area.

Other production processes result in the imposition of spillover costs on people not involved in either the production or use of the goods or services produced. For example, because no one in the past "owned" the rights to the atmosphere, steel producers and automobile owners emitted exhaust fumes into the atmosphere, adversely affecting many who did not benefit directly from the steel or the automobiles. They suffered the external costs of eye irritation and strain and peeling paint on their houses. Since producers and consumers of steel do not bear the full cost of production, the product is underpriced and oversold. That is, since the price of the product is less than its true cost, consumers are buying units of goods that are not to them really worth the true costs.

Although producers may be concerned about the deterioration of the environment due to collective pollution, none has, in a highly competitive market, an economic incentive to do anything about it. Indeed, if one firm buys pollution abatement equipment, its costs will be higher than its competition's. It will have to charge a higher than market price and will be undercut in the market. Given the economic fate of all producers and consumers if they attempt to remedy the pollution problem *individually*, they can be expected to continue polluting. Adherents of the externality argument conclude that spillover costs can be remedied by (1) the assignment of private property rights to the atmosphere, (2) government regulation of the emission of pollutants, or (3) imposition of a government tax on the product. The central problem with pollution is that too much of some goods is produced, and too little of other goods is produced. An excise tax on a good creating the pollution increases its price and, therefore, shifts consumer purchases away from it to other goods (which presumably do not have external costs associated with them). In this way, so the argument goes, government intervention in a private market with a specially tailored excise tax can improve market efficiency.

In the restricted sense specified by economic theory, externalities are an economic raison d'être for government. Externalities can be and have been used to explain public provision of basic law, police protection, roads, education, and systems of justice. Throughout much of economic literature, market externalities are presumed to define the scope and boundaries of government. The implicit assumption is that government *resolves* problems of externality instead of creating additional ones that must be corrected by further government action. In short, economic analysis presupposes that government, by intervening in private markets, does not extend the case for its own existence. However, as can be shown with several concrete examples, this is not the case. Economic theoreticians have, because of intellectual myopia, failed to see the self-perpetuating dimensions of their own argument for government.

THE SELF-PERPETUATING GOVERNMENT

Examples of how government actions have spillover (external) effects and give rise to further extensions of government abound. The following is a nonexhaustive but representative list.

Automobile Insurance

Reckless driving by some drivers imposes spillover costs on nearby drivers. Nearby drivers incur the greater risk of having a wreck and incurring the cost of personal injury and damage to their cars when accidents occur. According to the economic justification for government, it is, therefore, a legitimate function of government to specify requirements for driver's licenses, speed limits, and other rules of the road. In addition, the government can legitimately require all drivers to carry car insurance. Insurance premiums, however, depend on such factors as the accident rate, the severity and cost of injuries, and the cost of replacement parts for cars. In turn, the accident rate is a function of, among other things, the amount of liquor and drugs drivers consume, the level of drivers' education, and the mechanical condition of automobiles. The cost of injuries varies with doctor and hospital fees, which depend on the prices of a host of resources, and so forth.

A change in the price of medical services or replacement parts, or in the educational level of drivers can affect insurance premiums. In the absence of governmentally required automobile insurance, such changes would be the types of consideration a person must include in calculating whether to continue an insurance contract. In completely private markets, no one is forced to continue purchasing insurance: every individual can adjust personal expenditures and seek a new equilibrium when market changes occur. However, when government forces people to buy insurance as a condition of owning and operating an automobile, the choices are immediately and severely restricted. The political process sets the amount of premiums. As economist Richard Ippolito found, nonreckless drivers subsidize reckless drivers, even when there are special rate classifications for reckless drivers.[6] This is to be expected when nonreckless drivers cannot drop their policies and turn to a company that refuses to insure reckless drivers. Therefore, reckless drivers do not have to pay the higher rates necessary to entice a private firm to give them a policy. In addition, when rates go up, people cannot buy more or less insurance and, thereby, buy themselves into a new equilibrium. People must make structural changes: they must either stop driving altogether or move to another state or country.

Under state-mandated insurance systems, individual policyholders are in essentially the same economic position as persons affected adversely by industrial smoke. They must incur a cost—higher premiums—when the amount of reckless driving in the population increases or when people increase their consumption of booze and have more wrecks. Like polluters, reckless drivers impose an external cost on the rest of the driving population. To reduce the externalities created by requiring automobile insurance, government can justify, *on economic grounds*, the further extension of its authority. It can rationalize government regulation of liquor consumption, automobile safety through inspection systems, and medical expenditures for injuries. Furthermore, since the cost of automobile parts affects insurance premiums, the government has an argument for the regulation of automobile production. Since doctor and hospital fees influence automobile insurance premiums, the government can justify extending its service into regulation of the medical industry; indeed, it can argue for government production of subsidized medical services. If the government carries the analysis to its logical conclusion, it can justify the regulation of suppliers of the automobile and medical industries on the grounds that their cost structures have spillover costs that affect insurance policyholders.

Although at some point the external effects of private actions cease to affect insurance premiums, recognition of the logical extremes to which government action could go suggests that as automobile travel increases, the external consequences of any class of actions increases. Accordingly, as travel grows, the argument for extending the domain of government becomes progressively more reasonable on economic grounds. In terms of an input-output matrix of the economy, required automobile insurance could possibly lead to the regulation of the entire economy.

Agricultural Aid

Although it requires imagination, an economic justification for governmental aid to farmers can be developed. Consider a frequently heard argument. Because agriculture plays an important economic role and instability in agricultural markets causes instability in most other markets, agricultural stability is a quasi-public good that can be efficiently produced only by government intervention in the form of price floors or production controls. Besides, it may be argued, small family farms are an important component of American culture. If family farms go the way of horse and carriage producers, all America will be the poorer. Again, the argument attaches public-good characteristics to the farming industry and creates an economic case, as poor as it may seem, for governmental intervention.

Government agricultural programs, however, have tended to raise the price of food. To correct for this economic problem, which hits the poor especially hard, the government can justify, as it has, the subsidization of the poor's food budget. Taxpayers, then, not only pay to buy surplus agricultural products (if a price support system is used) but also subsidize food stamps. Because of governmental intervention in farm markets, agricultural productivity, as well as the cost of fertilizer, seed, and equipment, influences agricultural markets and, secondarily, tax rates. The government, therefore, has the economic justification it needs to control these secondary market effects, either by setting standards of production or by appropriate manipulation of taxes and expenditures. President Carter used this argument during the energy crisis of 1979 to justify special diesel fuel allocations to farms, another expansion of government control.

Police and Fire Protection

The external benefits of police protection are fully recognized. To the extent that the police deter crime in a given area, then all within that area benefit in terms of the lower risk of being a victim of a crime. People in the protected area benefit from police services whether they make any payment toward covering the cost or not.

Again, however, the provision of police services means that large classes of individual actions now have external effects. People who fail to lock their house or car or even to buy locks for their doors encourage crimes in their communities and cause police resources to be diverted from other uses or force an increase in the costs of achieving any given crime rate. Public provision of police protection means that many classes of individual actions generate, as in the case of automobile insurance, external costs. The public good of police protection is communal property, to be used (like the atmosphere) on a first come, first served basis at what approximates a zero price. As with any other communal property, available essentially free of charge, individuals tend to overuse and abuse the resources involved in the absence of further governmental action. Government, therefore, can use the same economic rationale for regulating the construction of houses, cars, and their locks as it uses for the provision of police protection.

Although it is possible to exclude nonpayers from the benefits of fire protection, fire protection has some of the same characteristics as police protection. Accordingly, fire departments are almost always provided through local government. People who have fires, however, impose a spillover cost on the rest of the community, especially if aid in the form of income assistance and hospital care is provided to fire victims. Because of fires, people in the larger communities pay higher taxes than they would otherwise. Communities throughout the nation have, like Clemson, South Carolina, used the externality argument to justify ordinances that require homeowners to install smoke detectors. The public good argument is also the basis of many building codes that specify permissible types of fire-retardant materials.

Disaster Relief

State and federal relief for victims of such natural disasters as floods, tornadoes, and earthquakes are justified on the grounds that charity is a public good that benefits virtually everyone who cares about the welfare of others. A completely free market, so the argument goes, results in less disaster relief than is socially desirable. Because disaster relief programs entitle flood victims to certain forms and levels of aid, an economic argument can be made for providing subsidized insurance against floods. The basic argument is that this encourages people to share in paying for their own disaster relief by purchasing insurance.

However, direct disaster relief, or subsidized insurance, reduces the costs that flood victims bear. This reduction in losses raises demand for property in flood-prone areas, increases the willingness of people to build in them, reduces people's incentive to remove property from threatened areas, and therefore enlarges the loss of property when floods occur. Again, individual actions, through their impact on damage claims and taxes, have external effects, rationalizing governmental regulation of construction in flood-prone areas, which it has done.

Welfare and Education

Unemployment compensation and welfare programs extend the scope of the government far beyond the needs of a "minimal state." The unemployed or impoverished are entitled to public assistance, which can come in various forms from food stamps to housing allowances to outright cash grants. Unemployment adds to the welfare burden of the state. Because education influences people's productivity and employability, the government can justify extending its influence into and over educational programs, providing educational facilities, and increasing the ease with which any form of "human capital" can be acquired. Many of the increases in state expenditures on education in recent decades are due not to the external benefits of education per se but rather to the governmentally induced external benefits of welfare programs. Education reduces the need for outright welfare expenditures and, supposedly, lowers, on balance, people's taxes. The statewide systems of technical institutes and community colleges that grew up in the late 1960s were, in part, a response to newly assumed welfare responsibilities of government.

Because of the externalities of welfare programs, day-care centers for working mothers have been instituted and expanded. Washington, D.C., has justified similar facilities in its junior and senior high schools on economic efficiency grounds. The contention is that teenage mothers unable to go to school because of their child will go onto welfare and unemployment roles. The city and ultimately the taxpayers will pay the bill. To prevent the development of such externalities, child-care centers, which at one time were a strictly private good, are provided as a public good.

Total Debasement of a Concept

During the 1979 energy crisis, singer John Denver had a 4,000-gallon gasoline storage tank installed on his property and ordered two more 2,000-gallon tanks. Environmental groups demonstrating in front of Denver's property complained that he was a hypocrite (he had several hit songs about the environment) and that if everyone were as greedy as Denver, the supply of gas would be seriously restricted and the price would skyrocket. They contended that all buyers would be hurt by the wealthy John Denvers of the world and concluded that the government has an obligation to prevent gasoline hoarding.

In effect, the protesters equated Denver's purchases with smoke pollution: both impose external costs on people not associated with them. Although in a sense correct, the protesters failed to see a critical distinction between the two acts. In the case of smoke pollution, the cost of producing some good is borne by people who have nothing to do with its production and use; the product, as a consequence, is under-priced and overproduced. Because of the technical nature of smoke as a component of production, the market sends out incorrect pricing signals, suggesting that the resources used in the good's production are not as scarce as they really are. (These types of external costs are, because of their nature, referred to in economic literature as "technological external costs"—truly a mouthful.)

Price increases due to growth in market demand or contraction in market supply are categorically different from smoke pollution. First, they do not involve the technical characteristics of pollution. Second, they do not distort pricing signals; they *are* the pricing signals. Third, they do not result in either under- or overproduction of any good like gasoline. Given the market price, whatever it is, people can still buy as much of the product as they wish so long as they pay the price that covers *all* costs of production. There was nothing in Denver's purchase that concealed or distorted production costs.

The market system tends to allocate goods to those who value them relatively more. Obviously, by buying the gasoline for storage, Denver indicated that he valued the product more than other people who, because the price was then pushed too high, did not buy it. Voila! The market performed its basis function.

No doubt, there are those who contend that gasoline storage is of no value. To them, maybe not; but obviously not to Denver, or else he would not have paid the price of installing the tanks. It is difficult to see why storing gasoline, which gives the owner a sense of security, should *a priori* be construed as any less valuable than a host of other uses, like running generators for ski lifts or going to and from work to make skiing equipment. Again, as the preceding chapters stressed, the free market gives people the freedom they need to buy what they want; it ensures that the protesters outside Denver's property have no more right to force him to buy what they want him to buy than Denver has to force the protesters to buy what he wants them to buy. It keeps the would-be social dictators of the world off each other's backs.

Policymakers have repeatedly expressed concern over the effects that movements of market prices have on people. When interest rates go up, programs are instituted to subsidize the mortgage payments of low- and middle-income groups, the "victims" of the market. When the price of heating fuel increases, programs are hurriedly designed to ensure that the elderly are not unduly hurt. When medical costs rise, national health insurance programs are offered as a means of helping virtually everyone because "no one can afford to get sick any longer." To the extent the public accepts such claims, the notion of external costs is corrupted. If we continue to accept such arguments and fail to see the folly in them, there is no limit to the bounds of government: the government can intervene in the marketplace any way it wants because markets are critically dependent on price movements for disseminating information about the relative scarcity of goods and resources. As preceding chapters have argued, individual freedom is intrinsically linked to the absence of government in markets.

BUDGETS AND EXTERNALITIES

The public provision of a good can give rise to governmentally created externalities because the actions of many people affect social expenditures and the amount of taxes the government must collect. This is a unifying theme in all of the examples cited. However, an important qualification needs to be added: the extent of the governmentally created externalities and, hence, the expansion of the legitimate domain of government depend critically on the existing size of the government sector.

A relatively small government means that any set of individual actions affects few government programs and, to only a limited extent, the taxes that people must pay. To consider the extreme case, if the government budget is only $1, the government by definition affects few people by the services it provides and by the taxes it collects. Given such a low budget, a change in the birthrate, to use a class of individual actions with interesting implications, affects few programs. The birthrate of the population can double, but people's taxes can remain virtually unchanged.

A relatively large government, on the other hand, must provide a sizable quantity and variety of public goods. Classes of individual actions can, therefore, significantly affect many programs and the tax burden of the general citizenry. Changes in the birthrate, for example, will affect public expenditures on hospitals since more beds will be needed; on schools since there will be more children to educate; on roads and garbage collection since there will be more miles traveled and more waste products to be removed from homes; and on welfare payments since more births can mean fewer working parents. Consequently, when government is large, an economic case for government control of the birthrate can be made more forcefully than when government is small. Put another way, to the extent that the economic justification for government influences the scope and size of government, the likelihood of governmental control of the birthrate (as well as many other classes of actions) is raised with an increase in the size and scope of government. To the extent that size of government affects the perception of the legitimate domain of government, the externality argument for government perpetuates expansion of government, at least up to a point.

Once government begins to break out of the confines of the minimal state defined by strict constitutional barriers to governmental expansion, growth in government can have a snowballing effect. The logical extreme may be, but not necessarily is, pervasive governmental, collective control of the economy. This analysis, at the very least, may explain much modern interest in national economic planning, as well as contemporary interest in publicly financed birth control programs and abortions.

THE PROPENSITY OF GOVERNMENT TO EXPAND

If government activities cause classes of individual actions to create externalities, then why is the externality problem not resolved by a contraction of government? Why is there a tendency for government to take on new responsibilities and to expand in size and scope? Several answers can be tendered. First, many voters do not recognize the cause of the externality problem. Externalities present complex conceptual and empirical problems for even well-educated and well-informed voters. Furthermore, politicians, bureaucrats, and potential beneficiaries of expanded government programs have a personal interest in making the general citizenry believe, correctly or incorrectly, that the inefficiency created by the new externalities can be remedied at very little cost or at a cost that is less than the value of the benefits.

Second, governmentally created externalities are spread, through the budget and tax system, over a large number of people, no one of whom is affected much by the externalities. The general population has little incentive even to learn about the source of the new external costs they bear, much less become sufficiently active in politics to increase significantly the probability that the scope and size of government will be reduced. On the other hand, a relatively small group of beneficiaries of expanded government programs will have a significant stake and interest in seeing government grow. These people will tend to be much more politically active than the general population. The uneven balance of political activism between those who want expanded government and those interested in reducing the size of government fosters a political bias in favor of government expansion.[7]

Third, the externality of a given set of individual actions like births can be due to a number of government programs. When pieces of legislation are considered separately, the cost of passing legislation that will control, say, the birthrate, can be lower than the cost of cutting back a number of other government programs. For example, it may well be more economical to legislate a birth control program than to reduce the budget of an array of government welfare and educational programs and thus eliminate the rationale for public support of birth control programs. Again, a political bias, based on economic considerations, may favor government expansion. The expanded size and scope of government becomes "locked in," which increases the likelihood of further government expansion.

Contemporary society seems to be ensnared in a seductive, inexorable expansion of government. Describing the consequences of this is far easier than exploring its causes. This chapter has attempted to explain the expansion of government as the result of the emegence and general acceptance of new intellectual movements in economics. Without question, other intellectual movements in other disciplines are partially to blame. However, the examples presented suggest one major point: important new ideas are often distilled in the rarified world of universities, think tanks, and government bureaucracies. Their creators often assume that "good men" will do "good things" if given "good theory"; that seems to have been an article of faith to Keynes. However, before new intellectual movements are set afoot, their long-term political implications must be evaluated. We must know where they will lead—how and to what extent they may be corrupted by imperfect people in a political setting. Constitutional constraints on government force policymakers to take the long view and protect the political process from "madmen in authority" who have distilled *their* frenzy from academic scribblers of just a few years back.

The Dynamic Duo:
Free Speech and Free Markets

People like you and me, though mortal, of course, like everyone else, do not grow old no matter how long we live. What I mean is that we never cease to stand like curious children before the great Mystery into which we are born. This interposes a distance between us and all that is unsatisfactory in the human sphere— and this is no small matter. When, in the mornings, I become nauseated by the news the New York Times *sets before us, I always reflect that it is anyway better than the Hitlerism that we only barely managed to finish off.*

Albert Einstein
Letter to Julius Berger

CHAPTER 7

It was one of several political cartoons carried on the editorial page of a midwestern paper one July Sunday in 1979. The name of the paper has been forgotten, but the cartoon is too graphic to forget. Five vultures were perched in a row on a limb of a large denuded tree; the head of a Supreme Court justice—Burger, Stewart, Stevens, Rehnquist, and Powell—topped each avian body. Below them lay the mutulated carcass of what was labeled the First Amendment. The vultures were obviously satisfied with their meal.

The justices caricatured that Sunday had not too many weeks before formed the deciding majority in *Gannett Company, Inc.* (the country's largest newspaper chain) v. *DePasquale.*[1] In that case a lower court had precluded the press access to the records of a pretrial hearing. The Supreme Court, in agreeing with the lower court, ruled that the right of a defendant to a fair trial outweighed the constitutional right of the press and public to access to the proceedings. The cartoonist, as well as editorial writers around the country, was outraged by the decision, suggesting in his work that once again the Supreme Court had abridged the press's basic First Amendment rights.

Earlier in the year the Supreme Court made another important ruling against the press in *Pennington* v. *Kansas.*[2] In investigating a murder, a newspaper reporter cited an unidentified source who claimed he had heard a third party threaten the murder victim's life. The attorneys for the defense wanted the name of the source, but the reporter refused to divulge it, claiming First Amendment protection under the Constitution. A lower court held the reporter in contempt. Again, the Supreme Court reasoned that the rights of the defendant to a fair trial outweighed, on balance, any rights the press might have to confidentiality. The decision stunned the press.[3]

In reporting on *Gannett* for *Newsweek*, Aris Press and Diane Camper wrote with a tempered sense of moral indignation: "Most Americans have assumed that secret trials have no place in their judicial tradition. Evils perpetrated behind the locked doors of the British courts led the Founding Fathers to guarantee public criminal trials in their new Constitution, and a courtroom where every person can be judged openly by his peers has become a symbol of freedom." Their report gave considerable prominence to the comments of Allen Neuharth, president of Gannett Company, who quipped, "I have no hesitancy in saying that the majority of the Supreme Court has indicated that they consider the judiciary to be a private club. They're signaling, 'Your chambers and your courtroom belong to you, not to the public.' " And Press and Camper concluded their story (not editorial) with a cheap moralistic shot, "Few journalists can realistically expect the court to find them privileged characters. For the moment, the press has been put on the same level with the citizenry it seeks to enlighten."[4] We must ask: Did the Founding Fathers intend the press (which is composed of people) to be on a social and legal pedestal separate from the "commoners"?

Again, in mid-1981 the Supreme Court handed down its decision in the case of Philip Agee, who in 1974 began a campaign to damage the CIA and to reveal the names of CIA agents. Cyrus Vance, secretary of state in the Carter administration, had in 1979 revoked Agee's passport for violating the contract that Agee had freely signed with the CIA and that restrained Agee from talking about his work. In a 7-2 decision the Supreme Court upheld Secretary Vance's revocation of Agee's passport; and ". . . [F]or the next 48 hours," wrote columnist James Kilpatrick, "a bystander might have believed the sky had fallen. The *New York Times* and the *Washington Post* erupted with moans and goans. A huddle of Harvard professors collapsed in heaves and sighs."[5] According to many in the press, the Supreme Court ruling that summer day was a clear violation of the press's First Amendment protection: the ruling would have a chilling effect on the willingness of people to dissent against the government.

The important issue here is not the legal correctness of any particular Supreme Court decision. Rather, it is the dual attitude of much (but not by any means all) of the press (and much of the public) toward government regulation. On the one hand, the press, in general, as evidenced by its predictable reaction to recent Supreme Court decisions, has an obvious disdain for any suggestion that its activities be clipped, restrained, or regulated by government. It clings tenaciously and justifiably to the freedoms articulated for it in the Constitution. The First Amendment is a part of the press's professional armor—deservedly so.

On the other hand, a significant portion of the press is often among the first to point out the need for government regulation of this or that industry. Reporters would object strenuously to any requirement that they divulge their sources, open their newsrooms to search by the police, testify before grand juries, turn over their notes to courts, and restrict what they write. But many of these same reporters see no harm in government's requiring other industries to divulge sensitive information relating to their products, to meet officially established standards, to pay in accordance with legal minimum wage rates, to design facilities to meet government safety standards, and to charge the prices set by government fiat.

Much of the press assumes that there is a clear philosophical, categorical distinction between its activity and the activities of other industries. But, as this chapter argues, this distinction is completely arbitrary. Such vagaries make a poor foundation for a social philosophy of government.

In recent years, the highest levels of government have, on occasion, echoed and compounded the philosophical confusion of the press. President Carter, for example, frequently expressed considerable concern for the state of "human rights" at home and abroad. Just what he meant by human rights was not completely clear. However, he did seem to fancy that there was a legitimate conceptual distinction between the rights of free speech, press, religion, and democratic participation and the rights of free markets. Because of his concern, President Carter was *rightfully* willing to jeopardize, by citing human rights violations, our political relationships with countries like South Korea, the Soviet Union, South Africa, Iran, and Nicaragua. In my view, his intentions should, on the whole, be applauded. However, he showed little reluctance to impose "voluntary" wage and price controls on the entire economy and add willfully to the compound rate of growth in government regulation.

These inconsistencies highlight some basic questions: Can a conceptual distinction be made between "human rights" and "property rights"? Are not the arguments for freedom of speech, press, and religion similar (if not identical) to the arguments for freedom of markets? The purpose of this chapter is to address such questions head on; it is not to question the legitimate concern people have for human rights. Rather, its intent is to argue, as forcefully as possible, that market rights are also human rights; that market rights, too, are legitimate human concerns.

PERCEIVED DIFFERENCES

Most people in the press and in society's elite intellectual circles who favor freedom of speech and the press and, at the same time, advocate government control of various industries seem to imagine that the material of their labor differs substantively from the products of other private enterprises. They deal in "ideas," so the argument goes; others produce more mundane goods and services, "material" that appeals to the flesh and the senses, not the cerebrum. They view freedom of speech and press, but not the freedom of the market, as an extension of freedom of thought. Ideas are ideas: elusive, ephemeral, and difficult to regulate without controlling human thought itself. Goods, on the other hand, are goods: identifiable, tangible, largely distinct from thought itself. Ideas are creations of the human mind (and spirit), and they are important because of the (presumed) uniquely human capacity of thought and reason. Freedom to think and reason, so the argument may be developed, is necessary if people are to be human and not just animal. Goods and services, however, embody real-world resources that other animals share, although in other forms.

This presumed distinction between free speech and free markets is misleading at best and a gross distortion of the facts at worst. The production of a good like furniture requires many resources—land, material, labor, and capital. But the fruits of the press (or any other intellectual discourse) are also products of long and complicated production processes involving the use of many resources like gasoline, textiles, food, electricity, and telephone communications, which are subject to extensive government controls. Indeed, the final product of the press appears to be far more physical than the final product of an electric power company or of a psychological counseling service. Any good reporter understands that it takes time (labor) to gather the facts of a story, to mold them into an article, and to see them through the newsroom to the newsstand. A good deal of capital—real and financial—is involved in making free speech and press a meaningful social phenomenon. The press is a capitalist enterprise dependent on the capitalist system! How free would the press be if ownership of all pressroom production facilities were not private? If all property were controlled by government, free speech would not be worth the paper it is printed on.

True, the final product of the press incorporates ideas that at times concern the most critical issues of our age. The press provides an invaluable public forum for evaluating these issues. However, so-called material goods and services also embody ideas that are often no less critical to people's welfare than the ideas on the front page of the morning newspaper. Consider the complexity of the ideas incorporated into the design and construction of an automobile, a building, or a toaster. Is there any intrinsic reason that ideas inked on newsprint should qualify for any greater protection from government controls than the ideas incorporated into the structure of a garment, a bicycle, or a home? My purpose in indicating the similarities of "ideas in print and speech" and "ideas in goods" is not to defame freedom of the press and speech (as well as religion). Quite the contrary, it is to suggest that freedoms of the market should be accorded much the same government protection as our political freedoms—for they also are largely political freedoms.

FREE SPEECH AS A SOCIAL HAZARD

Advocates of free speech and government control of other production processes sometimes argue that goods and services produced by private industries can be harmful to people's health and general well-being. Indeed, they can kill. Cigarettes and guns are good examples. Hence, government must protect people from these goods and services, from the abuse of those who would use unrestricted market freedom to their own advantage.

As intuitively appealing as the argument sounds, it falls flat as a justification for a differential social approach to the control of speech and markets. Freedom of speech and press, like cigarettes, can also be hazardous to people's health—and no less deadly than many mundane material goods and services. People have died because someone stood up in a crowded theater or stadium and yelled "fire" or because the press reported strategic military and intelligence information. (Consider the deaths of the CIA agents whose names were revealed by the press under the constitutional protection of the First Amendment.) The Reverend Jim Jones, through his own exercise of the freedoms of speech, press, and religion, led more than nine hundred of his followers first to Guyana, then (with a little coercion) to their suicidal deaths. Many murderers acquired their only instruction in how to kill from television. Social expressions of freedom of speech, press, and religion are often deadly. Sometimes, extraordinarily deadly! Hitler and others like him rose to power partially because they were free to speak and to convince others, through print and oratory, that they were the true light and salvation of their times. These instances of abuse of First Amendment rights are not cited to undermine the legitimacy of fundamental rights. On the contrary, the intent is to place the case for all freedoms—including market freedoms—in proper perspective.

COMPETITIVE IDEAS AND MARKETS

One of the strongest arguments of proponents of basic First Amendment rights is: "We do not know which ideas are 'right' when any issue is first discussed. Indeed, we do not even know what issues, out of the whole range of issues, warrant public consideration. People must have the freedom not only to speak their own minds but also to listen to others. They need to hear all competing ideas not only because they will be well informed on the range of issues, but also because they will be in a reasonably good position to evaluate competing issues and choose the best course of action under the circumstances."

If this argument is intended to show that freedom of speech is distinct from freedom of markets, it is, again, seriously flawed. We understandably think of markets as dealing with things because things are readily observable. However, we could just as easily view markets as processes by which ideas, incorporated in things, are traded. Indeed, as previous chapters pointed out, socially recognized rights to do things are the real substance of trade. Furthermore, as with freedom of speech or religion, we often cannot identify, beforehand, the particular ideas embodied in goods and services wanted by most people. We must allow an individual the freedom to test his ideas in order that he may learn what goods and services, from a whole range of potential goods and services, are actually preferred. In short, a free market is, like free speech, a competitive process in ideas. We need both freedoms for essentially similar reasons.

Some seem to think that freedom of speech takes pre-eminence over other freedoms because freedom of speech is necessary in order to prevent any one person from having control over what ideas are actually considered and what courses of action are actually taken. Freedom of speech, it is argued, gives everyone some power to speak his or her mind, ensuring as best we can that no idea is accepted solely because it is the only alternative available. The freedoms of speech, press, and religion are social means of decentralizing the power that some have over others. By giving people the freedom to speak, we deny people the freedom to coerce others to think or accept any particular ideas. We ensure, through First Amendment rights, that courses of action are *voluntary* in the sense that they are chosen in a competitive market of ideas. We deny government the right to restrict the freedom of speech simply because we want to deny some people (those who would govern) the rights to impose their ideas on us. As preceding chapters argued extensively, the case for the free market has the same philosophical basis: free markets limit the power of people to coerce one another; they allow for competition and, therefore, voluntary actions. Free, unregulated markets are a means of delimiting the monopoly power of government to determine what goods and services we each will have.

FREEDOM TO MOVE GOVERNMENT

Opponents of the free market suggest that freedom of speech means little if speech cannot be used to influence government to accept a particular policy course, such as restricting the scope of market activities through regulation. They may contend with good intentions that in a democracy everyone has a right to voice an opinion and everyone must accept the verdict of the "competition of ideas" worked out through the political process. This position reveals a gross confusion of basic issues.

In its purest form, freedom of speech is a means of restricting the power of people, of attempting to ensure as much as possible that coercion is minimized. Freedom of speech means the freedom to persuade, not to coerce; to elicit voluntary cooperation, not to impose one's will on another. If voluntarism were not the complement of freedom, then freedom would be greatly restricted because most everyone would seek to use his freedom to coerce others. It would be "back to the jungle" with a vengeance. To make freedom of speech meaningful, the scope of democracy must necessarily be restricted. Otherwise, freedom of speech can easily translate into a coercive power that one person or group, through the state, uses on others.

Granted, no nation can effectively organize without some government and some issues must be decided by democratic means. That point is well taken and forms the heart of much that has been written. The point here is relatively simple: as the scope and size of government are extended, the freedom of some people to speak and win in the political arena with less than unanimous agreement translates into government force and a loss to others of freedom from coercion. As government expands, the unanimity of agreement, so necessary to social tranquility, over government policy must evaporate; disagreement will become the hallmark of social discourse; freedom of speech will take on a coercive quality.

Many factions of society now harbor serious resentment toward the press. Both the political left and political right denigrate it for its failure to report the "truth." This resentment is quite understandable and predictable. Its freedom to print what it considers news is interpreted by others, now that government is large and expensive, as the power to influence public events and, thereby, as the power to coerce.

Journalist William Cheshire has written, "The press is powerful—more powerful than in any previous period in all history—and power and humility are strangers."[6] The unchecked power of the press and public skepticism toward it derive, I suggest, from the unchecked power of the government and the ability of the press to set the national political agenda and, in that way and to that extent, to influence and manipulate the government's power. Surely, the press would have less power than at present and people would be less concerned about the accuracy of news reporting if government were small and inconsequential. When government is constrained in what it can do, there are few public policies the press can influence by accurate or innaccurate reporting; there is little the press can do to affect taxes or budget allocations.

Freedom of the press is in some jeopardy these days. Many, no doubt, advocate restriction of the freedom of the press simply as a means of controlling the power that some people, the press, have over others through government. Alternately, we can advocate restrictions on the size and scope of government to achieve the maximum freedom of speech, press, religion, and other basic rights with diminished fear that those rights will be misused. We need restriction on government in the economy to preserve all basic freedoms. The connection between constitutional government and all our freedoms—including freedom of enterprise and freedom of speech—is inextricable.

MARKET CONTROLS AND FREE SPEECH

Almost all supporters of free speech see its suppression as a denial of valuable information that people need to conduct their daily lives effectively. It can be argued with equal vigor, however, that the suppression of market forces by government controls also muffles valuable information that should be available to the public. It is, in short, a gross form of censorship, as Walter Wriston, chairman of Citicorp, has poignantly observed:

> The American press would not tolerate for one moment an attempt by the government to suppress news of riots or political demonstrations on the grounds that it wants to "insure domestic tranquility." The press knows a threat to the First Amendment when it sees one.
>
> There are ten amendments in the Bill of Rights, although sometimes it seems that the press is so busy defending the first one that it is hard to get equal time for the other nine.
>
> Let me recall one of them—the Ninth Amendment—which few people ever read any more, let alone defend. It says: "The enumeration in the Constitution of certain rights shall not be construed to deny or disparage others retained by people." Is something being disparaged when the government's chief inflation-fighter tells a group of businessmen, as he did recently in Chicago, that "We will, with a degree of enthusiasm that I suspect many of you may consider unseemly, identify the miscreants [those who violate President Carter's 'voluntary' wage-price guidelines] publicly."?[7]

When the Department of Energy sends out agents with binoculars to spy on filling station operators to ensure that they are not "overcharging," as it did in 1979, government is engaging in a form of censorship. Would the press not be outraged if similar surveillance were directed at it? When government becomes large and expansive, as it has, does it not begin to dominate the flow of information and acquire a de facto power of censorship simply by its prominence in the total production of information?

The problem of government control of information is by no means trivial. In reporting on a General Accounting Office study of government information activities and on the public relations activities of only 48 agencies, *U.S. News & World Report* concluded that "the federal government spends more money each year trying to influence the way people think than it spends altogether for disaster relief, foreign military assistance, energy conservation, and cancer research."[8] The Watergate era has led many people to believe that the press is constantly dogging the federal bureaucracy for information that the latter does not want to see the light of day. Solid investigative reporting does occur. However, as columnist Joseph Kraft has pointed out,

> In the typical Washington situation, news is not nosed out by keen reporters and then purveyed to the public. It is manufactured inside government, by various interested parties for purposes of its own, and then put out to the press in ways and at times that suit the sources. That is how it happens that when the President prepares a message on crime, all the leading columnists suddenly become concerned with crime. That is how it happens that when the Air Force budget comes up for consideration, some new plane will streak across the continent in record time.[9]

And, it may be added, presidents now take annual vacations, for example, down the Mississippi on an old paddle-wheeler, for one simple purpose: to manage the news.

A first draft of a report, itself kept secret for a time, by the Commission on Federal Paperwork reiterated an important point: "Information within an agency is controlled and released only when the agency believes that the release will help accommodate agency goals . . . If this trend continues, it appears likely that the information resources—at one time defined as a free resource similar to air, water, and land—will be increasingly regulated by the federal government."[10]

FREEDOMS AS PRINCIPLES

The freedoms of speech, press, and religion are very important. Nothing said here is intended to deny that. On the contrary, I have attempted to show that the case for the free market is quite similar to that for free speech. In the words of University of Chicago Professor Ronald Coase,

> I do not believe that this distinction between the market for goods and the market for ideas is valid. There is no fundamental difference between these two markets and, in deciding on public policy with regard to them, we need to take into account the same considerations. In all of these markets, producers have some reason for being honest and some for being dishonest; consumers have some information but are not fully informed or even able to digest the information they have; regulators commonly wish to do a good job, and though often incompetent and subject to influence of special interests, they act like this because, like all of us, they are human beings whose strongest motives are not always the highest.[11]

Our rights under freedom of speech and freedom of markets are limited. They must be. Otherwise, it is back to the jungle. In the case of free speech, unlimited freedom for all would make the world resemble a Tower of Babel, with no one able to communicate effectively with anyone else. In the case of free markets, unlimited freedom would mean nonexistent property rights and nonexistent markets. Unlimited freedom, therefore, is a contradiction in terms. Free speech and free markets are both means of socially restricting people to ensure that power is dispersed and that coercion is minimized.

Freedoms everywhere can be and have been abused. We have noted that the Reverend Jim Jones abused, in a sense, the freedom of speech. Abuse, however, does not make a sufficient case for abandoning freedom of speech or press or religion as guiding social principles. The press would be the first to admit to abuse of freedom within its own camp—but it would also be the first to defend vigorously the *principles* on which its activities rest. Principles, because of their very nature, cannot be judged—condemned or evaluated—by reference to narrow and limited social events. Principles can be judged only in terms of the broad sweep of history and the social necessities of imperfect people attempting to live together. Freedom of speech is intrinsically valuable—but it is also intrinsically practical, imperfect but practical. So is freedom of the market. Instances of abuse of market freedoms can easily be recounted. Those of us who seek to defend the market need not—indeed, should not—deny that fact. There are only two relevant questions: Has the free market served us well? And, is freedom of expression in markets just as important as freedom of expression in print?

The case for the free market is not a case for "no government intervention." Any suggestion to the contrary makes about as much sense as the suggestion that there is no circumstance under which freedom of the press needs to be curtailed. Freedoms and rights often collide and trade-offs are required. (Consider the cases of *Gannett* and *Pennington* briefly mentioned at the start of this chapter.) The case for the free market is an argument for a predisposition, a social proclivity, toward freedom and against control; for extraordinary caution in shaping government policy; and for the use of principles in the conduct of public policy. That is the way we interpret First Amendment freedoms; that is the way we need to interpret freedom of the market.

Why is much of the press antipathetic toward the free market? To some extent the answer is baffling. The press, more than any other institution, should understand the benefits of freedom and the dangers of restricting it. The opposition of some segments of the press to the free market may be due to their inability to understand sweeping social issues. After all, the primary focus of journalists' attention is on describing *immediate* events, those that occurred today or yesterday or may occur tomorrow. Members of the press are continually pushed, literally and figuratively, to get to the scene of the latest fire and to reduce complex situations to a few inches of newsprint or to 60-second spots on a nightly television news program.

Perhaps, many members of the press truly believe that they were anointed by the Founding Fathers with special privileges and special protection from the coercive powers of government. To assume such an attitude, however, the press must overlook the Fifth and Ninth Amendments, as well as a series of court rulings during the early years of the nation that upheld market freedoms. Those members of the press who believe the Framers intended that they, the press, be given special protection simply because the words "free speech" are mentioned in the Constitution should realize that the Framers were intent upon using that document to contain the political process, not people's personal lives and the market. As Alexander Hamilton wrote in the *Federalist*, expressing his concern about the delineation of rights, "[T]he people surrender nothing; and as they retain everything, they have no need of particular reservations," to which he added:

> I go further, and affirm that bills of rights, in the sense and to the extent in which they are contended for, are not only unnecessary in the proposed Constitution, but would even be dangerous. They would contain various exceptions to powers not granted; and, on this very account, would afford a colorful pretext to claim more than were granted. For why declare that things shall not be done which there is no power to do? Why, for instance, should it be said that the liberty of the press shall not be restrained, when no power is given by which restrictions are imposed? I would contend that such a provision would confer a regulatory power; but it is evident that it would furnish, to men disposed to usurp, a plausible pretense for claiming that power.[12]

Perhaps, the press's opposition to the free market may also be due to the realization of reporters and editorial writers that they are indirectly competing with other industries for the attention and spendable income of the general public. Like all competitors, the press may be intuitively driven to suppress its rivals. By pushing for the enactment of protective and destructive regulation of other industries, the press can raise the relative prices of other (competing) goods *and* reduce the relative prices of its own products, thus increasing the demand for its services, raising its income, and elevating its social importance.

Perhaps, the reason for the opposition to free markets among segments of the press is even less benign. Journalists may implicitly recognize that the market represents a bound on government and, hence, a bound on the power of those who would use government. By destroying the predisposition of the general public to respect and rely on market processes, some members of the press may consciously envision the enhancement of their own power. In other words, the press may be antagonistic toward the free market because the market represents a constraint on its own power. Many members of the press do seem to relish the attention they are given by groups who fear them and who seek to manipulate them (in order to guide and direct public debate over public policies). If this is the way members of the press think, then the game they are playing is a dangerous one. Journalists and others who live by First Amendment protection may think that government can be used to control every industry except the press.

That may not, in the long run, be the case. Power unleashed may be power difficult to contain.

Admittedly, there is nothing in the Constitution that specifically guarantees a free market. The Founding Fathers never used the term. Did they believe that First Amendment rights were in some way more important than the freedom of exchanges? Clearly, the answer is no. The whole of the Constitution was an attempt to check the power of the government and, thereby, establish the freedom of people to make those trades that they, not government, thought important. My colleague Hugh Macaulay suggests that special attention may have been given to freedoms of press, speech, and religion for one fundamental reason: historical evidence had taught not that those freedoms were more important, but rather were more vulnerable to violation by government. History has since proven the Founding Fathers wrong. Market freedoms are just as easily violated as political freedoms. Perhaps, as Macaulay suggests, we need to rewrite the First Amendment to include all basic freedoms.

The Return to a Free Economy

Alice: "Will you tell me, please, which way I ought to go from here?"

Cat: "That depends a great deal on where you want to get to."

Alice: "I don't much care."

Cat: "Then it doesn't matter which way you go."

Lewis Carroll
Through the Looking Glass

CHAPTER 8

The party was much like other faculty gatherings, polite but a little dull. From across the room, several people could be overheard. Given the level of their voices, they obviously meant for others to hear them. The subject was energy—what the president had done right, what he had done wrong, what he should have done. The common concern was the oil companies' "rip-off of the consumer." The criticisms were standard; the term "exploitation" was bandied about as though its definition were fixed in granite. An indignant comment from one of the group was particularly interesting: "That's our oil they are taking from the ground and making a profit on. God made it, the oil is ours, and we are having to pay dearly for it."

Such a declaration displays immense ignorance about the free market system. The speaker apparently had no understanding of the importance of property rights in giving people an incentive to produce what consumers want at the lowest possible cost. He did not realize that the same comment could be made about air, water, trees, fish, crops, iron ore, and human labor (even his). In addition, it was clear that he had little appreciation of the role the pricing system plays in organizing and directing people's behavior in a complex society. He, perhaps, believed production occurs spontaneously. He was openly in favor of freedom—academic freedom for himself and his colleagues. On the other hand, he was perfectly willing to place the oil companies in the straitjacket of government control and, perhaps, to nationalize the oil industry.

Those of us who think we understand the case for the free market system—indeed, a free society—can fret about the ignorance, banality, and utter stupidity displayed at the party. We can cast people like the professor off as "eggheads," suggesting that they are not in touch with reality. We can dismiss them or ignore them. We can call them a long list of names, some elegant, some vulgar. We can do all of this and more, but there is one thing we cannot deny: *the philosophical predisposition that characterized that evening's conversation guides much modern social politics.* Its logic may be absurd, but it is compelling to millions in this country, including our representatives in Congress and state legislatures.

The episode at the party reveals a social dilemma of no small importance. Those of us who support a free society want to cry out to the world, as did Martin Luther King, "free at last, free at last." We want others to understand what we understand, to know what we know, to feel as deeply about the absolute social necessity of the market system and constitutional government as we do.

But how do we persuade others that we are right when they feel just as strongly about their positions as we feel about ours? Our dilemma is made more acute by the lack of private incentive of many people to understand and promote the underlying logic of the free market economy. As stressed before, everyone has an interest in the formation of some minimal amount of government. The government can enforce the social contract that enables us to leave the jungle in which everyone may throw blows that hurt—hurt in terms of their physical impact and their economic impact. Everyone has an interest in declaring allegiance to the principle of "equality before the law," which is a way of ensuring that no one can use the power of the state for his own advantage. However, once the social contract is formed, everyone has an interest in being *more than equal*, in breaking the contract by enlisting the power of the state in the pursuit of narrowly conceived personal interests. Even those who understand the need for the social contract and for constraints on government have an interest in using the regulatory powers of the state to suppress their competitors and the taxing powers of the state to take income away from others for their own benefit.

Once the constraints on government are broken, all of us can be caught up in a competitive struggle for the use and abuse of government powers. Few may take the time to pause and reflect on what is happening to the social system as a whole. Those who do may be run over by the multitude who continue the struggle for use of government's power.

Why worry about the system when one is such an insignificant part of it? Why hold back from an attempt to manipulate government for one's own good? Why not do what all the rest do, farmers, truckers, barbers, military suppliers, doctors, college professors, real estate agents, and broadcasters? When constitutional barriers on government's powers crumble, why bother with such questions? Most of the calls for sanity in the conduct of government can be nothing more than the proverbial cries in the wilderness of a people resigned to playing the only real game in town, beggar thy neighbor.

Should we just give up? The answer, of course, is that we cannot; the stakes are too high. There are a few—a precious few—things that can be done, although their impact is necessarily uncertain. The "catch" described throughout this book demands that the quest for a free economy be pursued more or less simultaneously on several strategic fronts: constitutional, intellectual, and leadership. No free economy, if ever established, can long endure without considerable success in these areas. A free enterprise system corrodes from within unless there are constitutional bounds on government. But constitutional bounds are certain to crumble unless people have an intellectual appreciation of and moral commitment to the precept of individual freedom, the rights of private property, and the coordinating power of competition and the pricing system that go with freedom.

Proposed solutions to any social dilemma must spring from theoretical commentary. All proposals distilled from the idealized and rarified world of social thought should be inspired and venturesome; however, they must also be tempered by the realism of what seems timely and possible. Fortunately, the growth of government and the revelations of abuses of government power have given rise to a plethora of proposals for waging the constitutional, intellectual, and leadership battles. Because of their complexity, only summaries of the more promising proposals can be presented here. (See the citations for details of the arguments.)

CONSTITUTIONAL PRINCIPLES FOR A FREE ECONOMY

The Constitution is a document important for the *political* organization of the republic and the federal government. However, the following *economic* provisions need to be added to fortify the political provisions.

The Constitutional Equality of the Market

The Founding Fathers were intent on devising a market system that would act as a constraint on government. They presumed their views on that subject were clear, so much so that they sought to preserve, by very explicit language, the rights of religion, press, and speech. In writing a new constitution for the twenty-first century, Professor Hugh Macaulay suggests that the freedoms of the market be placed on equal footing with other basic freedoms. His new constitution reads in part, "Congress shall make no law abridging the freedoms of speech, press, religion, peaceful assembly, petitioning of government, *and* the market."[1]

Certainly, such a statement cannot keep the government out of every conceivable, imaginable market circumstance, just as the First Amendment has never been interpreted to mean that the government cannot, at times, violate a person's right to speak or write whatever he or she wishes. We recognize that in certain cases freedom of speech and press must be circumscribed by law. Hence, we understand the basis for laws that make yelling "fire" in a crowded, but nonburning theater a crime and the social legitimacy of laws against slander. However, the First Amendment has been important to orators and journalists alike because it created a legally binding presumption in favor of preserving the freedom of speech and against government intrusion on them. Professor Macaulay's suggestion should be taken seriously because it would create a legally binding presumption in favor of a person's right to engage in trades without government supervision and control. We need to assert the social need for guiding principles that will be violated only out of extreme necessity and not as a matter of course. The new constitution should induce us, once again, to take the "long view" and to judge, moment by moment, circumstances in terms of what we want for society in the centuries to come.

Tax Limitations

The Founding Fathers warned that we need to take "auxiliary precautions" in constructing a free society. They devised a series of organizational precautions against hasty approval of legislation. Admittedly, their list of things the federal government could do has been bent out of shape by aggressive and imaginative interpretation. However, they must have believed that the scope of the government would ultimately be restricted by its income. They could not have imagined the growth in the technology of tax collection, the modern importance of the personal and corporate income taxes (as well as a host of others), or the widespread use of tax deductions. Corporations were then rare, and the income of a corporation was not always divorced from the income of its owners. People's incomes were as ill-defined as the population; barter was common, cash transactions even more common; and payroll deductions were impractical. Besides, the Founding Fathers did not envision the federal government ever providing for much more than a system of justice and defense.

Given the increased sophistication in the technology of taxation, "auxiliary precautions" must now include fiscal constraints on government. The taxing authority of government must be strictly delimited. Recent tax-limitation movements in various states show promise of success because many recognize the need for political reasonableness and realism. One of the more promising proposals had been enacted in two states by 1980 and was likely to be enacted in several more states by the end of the 1980s. This proposal ties government tax revenues (or expenditures) to a certain percentage (say, 20 percent) of income.[2] This proposal has several notable advantages compared with other possible controlling rules.

First, it is a relatively simple and straightforward way of controlling and monitoring the size of government, easily comprehensible to the public. Second, it gives the government an incentive to administer its policies efficiently. The less obstructive (or the more constructive) the government is in the development of its economic policies for the private sector, the greater people's income and the greater the government's revenue. Third, the proposal links tax collections with income, population, and inflation. By denying to government the right to raise tax rates in reaction to transient economic difficulties, it will contribute to economic stability, enable citizens to plan better for the future, allow government to extend basic services like education to a growing population, and prevent government from benefiting from inflation.

Finally, such a scheme forces policymakers to perceive more readily that government is itself a scarce resource, constrained by scarce resources. Under the present system, in which government is more or less open-ended, there is little genuine competition among government bureaus for a relatively fixed quantity of resources. Any "overexpenditure" can be financed by increased taxes, including those generated by inflation. The public bears the burden of extended government programs in reduced real spendable income. Each bureau must be led to believe that a dollar spent on one program is not simply one less dollar available to the public, but one less dollar available for some other program under the bureaucracy's jurisdiction. It must perceive that, in a restricted sense, it bears a portion of the cost of its own aggressiveness in any area of social politics; it will, as a consequence, be led to produce more efficiently.[3]

The Balanced Budget Norm

Restricting tax collections alone, however, will not restrain the growth of government programs. Considerable government expenditures over past decades have been financed through deficit spending, borrowing, and running the printing presses. Hence, government's "fiscal constitution" should include provisions that control the government's ability to incur debt and to print money. As noted in earlier chapters, James Buchanan and Richard Wagner proffer a reasonable restriction: require the federal government to balance its budget.[4] The period of time over which a balance is required need not be the conventional fiscal year; the balanced budget requirement could be imposed for biennial budgets. The important point is that in order to control government expenditures effectively, the budgetary period must be relatively short.

The balanced budget requirement need not be uniformly applicable to all federal government expenditures. For example, federal parks financed exclusively by user charges could use that income (and not the full credit and taxing authority of the federal government) to pay back loans for capital expenditures. Lenders would have to accept the risk that user charges might be insufficient. In the event of default, the contract could specify that lenders would not then have recourse to the federal treasury. We must, however, be very careful in allowing for exemptions to the balanced budget norm. History has taught that government operators can be quite ingenious in using exemptions to circumvent the general intent of basic principles.

The Voting Rule

Government has expanded in the past because everchanging simple majorities in Congress have coalesced to pass programs that, though detrimental to others, are beneficial to the people who compose the majority at the time. Tax revenues have been pushed up to finance the total expenditures of the revolving majorities. But when the Constitution more or less restricts tax revenues, the various revolving simple majorities will be forced to bring total expenditures into line with the revenue available. One way of accomplishing that end is implied in the work of James Buchanan and Gordon Tullock: raise the majority required to pass a bill to, say, 70 percent.[5] This change would reduce the likelihood of passage of special interest legislation and increase the use of government revenues for truly public purposes.

Monetary Limitations

The power of the government to create money has been the source of much of its modern growth. The federal government has financed its way into economic prominence by creating money to buy what it wants.[6] Experience teaches that government can be effectively controlled only when government's money-creating power is severely circumscribed. Milton Friedman and Friedrich Hayek have offered specific proposals to this end. Friedman recommends that the growth of federal money (specifically, the "money base") be restricted to a certain percentage, say, 4 percent, a year.[7] He would, in short, deny the federal government the right to use its monetary powers to fine-tune the economy (which it cannot do anyway without making conditions worse) His proposal would also provide one additional check on the ability of the government to run budgetary deficits and to debase its outstanding debt by the inflation that inevitably follows overly aggressive money creation. Furthermore, this proposal would contribute to the long-run economic stability of the country by making the price level more predictable.

Hayek's proposal for monetary reform is more radical but still reasonable.[8] He and others suggest that we take from government its present monopoly control over money. One variant of such decontrol proposals would permit institutions other than government to create their own money—unfettered by government control. Under such a proposal, the federal government could maintain its own monetary system. Nothing in an open monetary system would prevent consumers from holding their liquid assets in strictly regulated federal dollars. If the growth in federal money were restricted (that is, if the value of federal money remained stable) and if the federal government efficiently supervised its own banks, there would be no reason (other than convenience) for people to hold nonfederal money.

However, an open monetary system would give people the freedom to choose which of several highly liquid assets they wished to hold; it would give people monetary options to which they could turn in the event federal money were corrupted by growth. An open monetary system would force the federal government to "compete" with other monetary suppliers to produce a stable medium of exchange. The demands of competition would, accordingly, temper the government's inclination to inflate prices. An open monetary economy would require free trade in various domestic moneys and, perhaps, a provision allowing tax payments in nonfederal money (at going market exchange rates).

Regulatory Limitations

The scope of government activity expanded considerably during the 1960s and 1970s through an extension of regulation of private markets and personal behavior—that is, through the imposition of costs on the private sector (a form of "implicit" or hidden taxation). Unless government regulation is controlled by constitutional means, government may continue to expand despite the imposition of fiscal and monetary limitations. To control the scope of government firmly, we should include an estimate of the costs (or implicit tax) of federal government regulation in the total tax collections of the federal government. This total must then be held to a specified percentage of income, as suggested above.[9]

Under such a provision, when policymakers impose a cost on the private sector through regulation, they will be forced to reduce expenditures on some government program financed by explicit taxes. This will induce more concern about the efficiency of regulatory efforts. When regulation is efficient, government's taxable income will expand along with national income. If, however, regulatory programs do nothing more than impose a cost on the private sector, the explicit tax income of the federal government will be reduced. The total cost of government borne by the private sector will remain constant.[10]

Regulatory Reform

A growing volume of technical research on the economic consequences of government regulation suggests that we need to do more than simply control the *growth* of future regulatory efforts. These studies have almost invariably concluded that regulation has resulted in market inefficiencies and, because of these inefficiencies, has reduced aggregate income below its potential.[11] This general conclusion appears to hold for such diverse industries as trucking, aviation, energy, agriculture, insurance, electric utilities, taxicabs, real estate, and drugs. The existence of regulation on such a broad scale has, accordingly, been explained by "distributional effects," that is, by the benefits received by those who have the necessary political support to acquire governmental protection from competition.[12] Similarly, political opposition to *deregulation* has been explained by the diffusion of the potential benefits of deregulation over a large number of consumers who have little incentive to make their views known to their political leaders and the concentration of costs on a relatively small number of producers who have considerable incentive to oppose political efforts to deregulate their individual industries.

Opposition to deregulation is, understandably, opposition to wealth transfers: although supplies may increase, deregulation of natural gas, for example, might cause a transfer of wealth from, say, the owners of natural gas and electric homes (who would have to pay higher prices for gas and experience a drop in the resale value of their homes) to gas companies. In the case of deregulation of taxicabs, the wealth transfer would be from taxicab owners (whose fares are being held artificially above competitive levels by regulation) to passengers. In the case of deregulation of the trucking industry, the wealth transfer could be from truck owners to their customers.

To return to a freer economy, we need to devise ways of breaking the inherent political opposition to deregulation. Economists have two recommendations: (1) a tax-compensation scheme and (2) a broad-based proposal to deregulate many industries at one time. The tax-compensation proposal couples deregulation of a particular industry with compensation for those who lose wealth in the process. The revenue for compensation payments is obtained from taxes levied on those who gain wealth. Since deregulation will increase aggregate income, all parties can (at least theoretically) be made better off by a tax-compensation scheme. However, the sheer complexities of computing the distribution of the tax burden and the compensatory payments have almost always made such schemes politically unattractive.[13] Furthermore, this proposal extends the government's taxation-subsidy role in the economy and is objectionable on those grounds alone. We must remain suspicious of what government would do with such authority.

Alternatively, net wealth transfers of deregulation (and, thereby, political opposition to deregulation) can be reduced by deregulating several industries at once. Those who lose from the deregulation of, for instance, natural gas, can be partially compensated for their wealth losses by the benefits they receive from deregulation of the trucking and other industries. Those who lose from the deregulation of the trucking industry can be partially compensated with benefits received from the deregulation of agriculture, banking, and insurance and the elimination of tariffs on imported goods. If each deregulation proposal is considered in isolation from all other proposals, it can provoke intense political opposition and little active support. However, if several deregulation proposals are considered as a *constitutional* package, then conceivably all can pass. (At the very least, the likelihood of passage can be enhanced.) People may lose from the deregulation of a particular industry, but they can gain, on balance, from the improvement in their purchasing power. In short, a return to a relatively free economy must be approached as a constitutional endeavor because free trade makes sense to the diverse economic interests in our midst only as a constitutional principle—as a broad prohibition against the differential use of governmental powers to protect or promote the economic interests of any particular group.

THE INTELLECTUAL BATTLE

The people behind state and national movements to restrict the fiscal powers of government are not so naive as to believe that a rewriting of constitutions alone will preserve a free economy. Constitutional principles are not like rocks in a museum showcase; they must be developed by reasonable men and women in words that are ultimately open to interpretation. If a free economy is to be preserved, interpretations must be guided by an emotional appreciation for and intellectual understanding of what those words mean. Practically speaking, this means that those of us who advocate a free economy must show supporters of collectivism that constitutional constraints on government are in their own (private or altruistic) interests and in the interest of the groups they wish to aid by governmental-political means.

Academic economists across the country have gradually, persistently been chipping away at the case for governmental social reform by showing the inefficiency of an array of government programs, from trucking regulation to the minimum wage law to social security. Some reform proposals have been successful. More can be expected as people begin to see the pattern of results: that government action more often causes social problems than cures them. A free market economy can now be compared not with an idealized view of social harmony promoted by government, but with the existing, imperfect system by which government is exploited by many (including businessmen and women) in the pursuit of narrowly conceived interests.

The intellectual challenges to a free economy cannot be met simply by more education, especially more economic education. First, if more education means more public education, it becomes a proposal to restrict government by expanding government. That may be no solution at all. Second, part of the problem is convincing the educational establishment, including many nonmarket economists and economic educators, of the need to reduce the scope and size of government.

Third, the effectiveness of introductory economics courses in improving students' understanding of the economy has been studied extensively. Many changes in educational technology, like program study guides and computer-assisted instruction, have been introduced. The qualifications of economic instructors, in terms of degrees, are higher, and textbooks are more colorful and readable. However, much of the research conducted on the effectiveness of basic economics courses has produced one almost inescapable conclusion: the long-run economic literacy of students remains low and virtually unaffected by the efforts of economic educators. Despite some encouraging findings to the contrary, "the George Stigler hypothesis," which maintains that students who have and have not had economics cannot be distinguished statistically on the basis of their economic literacy five years after college, remains valid.[14] On the basis of several criteria, students who took introductory economics seem to be no more astute in economic policy matters than their counterparts who never stepped into an economics classroom.[15] Explanations for the ineffectiveness of economics instruction are varied, as varied as the interests and backgrounds of the researchers concerned with the issue. Some have suggested that many economists employed as teachers sport their degrees and publish articles but do not care about being effective teachers. Although the economics profession probably has its share of lousy teachers, many economists do care very much about what and how much their students learn. Other researchers suggest that teachers have no incentive to be effective in their classes. There is, no doubt, some truth to this position, but it is difficult to believe that all the failures of economic education can be summarized and dismissed by "lack of incentive."[16]

The failures of economic education may go much deeper. First, students are continually exposed to much economic nonsense reported on television as news and dramatized on a variety of entertainment programs.[17] According to television, inflation is caused by higher prices or, better, big business, companies that can be actually observed raising their prices. Similarly, government deficits stimulate the economy; and pollution results from private property since property owners have an inherent interest in exploiting their rights. Political corruption at home and abroad is caused solely by the briber, the private businessperson who pays the bribe, not the bribee, the government official who accepts (and may have sought) the bribe. Businesses make profits by charging exorbitant prices and extorting income from consumers who need gasoline, heating oil, and other daily necessities (trade is not mutually beneficial). And, finally, businesses collude only to exploit consumers, whereas workers strike to obtain a fair wage and humane working conditions. In summary, any positive influence of a semester course in economics is simply overwhelmed by often well-intended but subtle and pervasive forms of countereducation. To win the intellectual battle, people interested in changing the public's economic views must consider funding educational programs for the people with power to influence public opinion, that is, journalists, especially television journalists.

Professor Henry Manne and his colleagues at the Law and Economics Center (originally at the University of Miami, now at Emory University) have developed an economics program for the legal profession, which should be encouraged and duplicated for journalists. For many years Manne has run two- and three-week seminars for lawyers and judges who wish to learn economics (and other seminars for economists who wish to learn how the legal profession thinks). The intent of the seminars is not to indoctrinate (that would be counterproductive) but to explore the issues (which is all that can be asked). Similar seminars need to be developed for journalists and others in positions to disseminate information concerning the private economy. In 1981, the Center for Political Economy and Natural Resources at Montana State University made a first effort to hold economic seminars for the press. From my participation in that seminar, I am certain that economists can learn as much from journalists in terms of what the other is doing wrong as journalists can learn from economists.

Public support for economic education is often justified on the grounds that such education is a "public good," much like national defense: economic education improves people's economic literacy and, therefore, makes them more intelligent citizens. Its cost is covered by more efficient, less costly government policies. The main rationale for *public* support is that people, acting on their own, cannot be expected to pay the full cost of economic education when many, if not most, of the benefits are received by people other than the ones learning the economics. The problem with this argument is that it presumes that people, once educated in economics, have an incentive to retain what they have learned and to use what they have retained in the voting booth. In producing the public good of economically literate public decisions, students should not be expected to behave any differently from fishermen faced with the production of a lighthouse. To the extent that the public good argument is correct for economic literacy, we should expect most students to forget much of what they have learned, especially since it is contradicted repeatedly in what they read and hear on a daily basis.[18] When constitutional limitations on government are absent, we should expect them to vote in accord with their private interests, not necessarily in accord with the economic principles they learned in class. Despite economics training, textile executives are likely to vote for tariffs on textiles, space workers to vote for an expansion of the space budget, and farmers to vote for more aid to agriculture. We should not expect people in general to spend much time and money fighting the continual plethora of economic issues in Congress. The variety and complexity of the issues overwhelm even the most dedicated of citizens.

Economic education must be designed to train people to think about public policies not in isolation but in a constitutional framework—to make them aware that many issues can be solved by constitutional restrictions on government. In other words, an individual citizen may have no private interest in incurring the full cost of education when the stakes are simply a tariff on textiles (which costs him, as an individual, very little). He may have considerable private interest in learning economics in order to vote on a whole group of issues. The ineffectiveness of economic education is due, in part, to the *political framework* in which it is used. We need to change the political framework.

THE LEADERSHIP PROBLEM

The catch in restoring a free economy cannot be completely resolved by re-educating the general public and revising the Constitution. More is required. People can benefit from a return to a free economy, but there are costs involved in re-educating the public and getting constitutional principles accepted as legitimate social concerns. Considerable costs are involved in persuading others, many of whom appreciate the attributes of a free economy, to leave the sanctuary of the free-rider position and to accept the mantle of free-economy advocacy. Since the benefits of advocacy are general, no one may have the private incentive to bear the costs involved. There is, in short, the potential for a leadership vacuum. How can we get the ball rolling? The obvious answer may be disquieting to those who seek logical solutions: we simply must have leaders—people who, like the Founding Fathers, value freedom for its own sake and value it sufficiently to incur the costs of starting a movement of diverse and reluctant individuals. Those who lead must proclaim repeatedly what they practice.

Such leaders must convince others that freedom is a means to an end for individuals who want to improve what they, not the government, consider to be their lot. However, from the perspective of society, freedom must be more than a means. It must be a basic value, whose importance is asserted and reasserted. For any free society to endure, people must be willing to lay down their lives for certain basic values, one of which is freedom itself. If people do not believe in freedom from governmental coercion, then as each person endeavors to use government to control others, he in turn will be controlled by government (which is manipulated by others), and all will move further down the road to serfdom.

People must affirm and reaffirm the moral integrity of the individual and counteract, wherever possible, the tendency to classify others into groups and classes. Above all, they must affirm, despite all voices to the contrary, their own individuality. Anne Wortham, a black writer, did just that in a review of Alex Haley's *Roots*:

> Unlike Alex Haley and other nationally-, racially-, or ethnically-determined people, I stand not at the end of a tradition but in the midst of an exciting life process that is my own. The social history of my ancestors does not flow through my psyche as a domesticated animal carrying the instincts of its ancestors in its genes. I am a person, and persons are self-determined individuals—even when they deny the fact and behave contrary to it. I am not some sociological construct that has stepped out of the last chapter of Alex Haley's novel. I am me—myself—and I. There has been no one like me in existence before and there will be no one like me in the future. *I* am the sculptor of my soul's spirit; *I* am the carpenter of my self-esteem; and that is my pride.[19]

For too long, individualists have stood by, allowing others to recommend solutions based on an arbitrary division of an amorphous society into sections as though it were a pie on a kitchen counter. To that, advocates of a free economy should, like Ann Wortham, proclaim, "I am me—myself—and I."

People must be forever skeptical of anyone or any group that espouses the attainment of humanitarian goals through government. To those worried about the free-rider problem in private charities, the forthright reply should be, "What about all of the forced riders in government charities?" Admittedly, there may always be a need for limited, governmentally sponsored welfare programs. By the same token, one point must be reiterated: *the power of government to do good through force has limits.*

Further, people must insist that everyone be treated equally before the law: that is, any governmentally sponsored advantage given to one group must be automatically made available to everyone else. Truckers, for example, benefit from Interstate Commerce Commission regulations simply because the protection they receive is discriminatory, unavailable to everyone else. Truckers enjoy the benefits of both a captured market in their own industry and competitive, unregulated markets in many other industries. They like their position, of course, because the state works with their particular interest in mind. However, if every other industry received the same protection from competition, truckers would be worse off. Although they would receive monopoly profits (because of governmentally sponsored protection), they would have to pay monopoly prices for everything they purchase. The benefits of free trade (no government protection) can be appreciated fully only when the rule of law is applied equally to all.

Finally, advocates of a free economy in prominent business positions must stand ready to bend the ear of the media when some business group, like Lockheed or Chrysler, pleads for government aid in times of economic trouble. They must be willing to stand up for the basic principle of free enterprise as a social system and to cry foul when necessary. The public cannot be called on to accept the principles of private enterprise when business—especially big business—is unwilling to live by those same principles.

Now is the time for optimism! We have lived through a period in which people literally idealized government and what it could do. We no longer have to speculate on the consequences of expanded government. We have the record before us: high unemployment and inflation rates, along with a plethora of mucked-up social programs, all bought at the price of high taxes, constricted productivity growth, and restrictions on individual freedoms. Now, better than ever, we can clearly see what it is like to have an unconstrained government. It is a state of affairs that appeals to virtually no one. Even the poor are beginning to see that the welfare state was probably never intended for their benefit and that there is a better way. Perhaps, just perhaps, we will observe in the 1980s a new approach to government, one that recognizes three important principles: (1) the power of any government to do good is limited; (2) the expansion of governmental decision making reduces individual freedom; and (3) without constitutional constraints on government, the free market system contains the seeds of its own demise. There are considerable grounds for hope.

Notes

Chapter 1

1. Committee for Economic Development, Research and Policy Committee, *Economic Literacy for Americans: A Program for Schools and for Citizens* (New York, 1962), p. 9.

2. William E. Simon, *A Time for Truth* (New York: McGraw-Hill, 1978), p. 73.

3. Walter B. Wriston, *Warning: The Law May Be Hazardous to Your Health* (New York: Citicorp, 1977), p. 3.

4. Raoul Berger, *Government by Judiciary: The Transformation of the Fourteenth Amendment* (Cambridge, Mass.: Harvard University Press, 1977). For detailed historical discussions of the breakdown of constitutional bans on government intervention in the private economy, see Terry L. Anderson and Peter J. Hill, *The Birth of a Transfer Society* (Stanford: Hoover Institution Press, 1980) and Bernard H. Siegan, *Economic Liberties and the Constitution* (Chicago: University of Chicago Press, 1981).

5. James M. Buchanan, *The Limits of Liberty: Between Anarchy and Leviathan* (Chicago: University of Chicago Press, 1975).

6. Wilhelm Ropke, *A Humane Economy: The Social Framework of the Free Market* (Chicago: Henry Regnery, Inc., 1960), p. 125.

7. Cited in Lino A. Graglia, *The Supreme Court's Busing Decision: A Study of Government by the Judiciary* (Los Angeles: International Institute for Economic Research, 1978), p. 7.

8. Shirley Letwin formally made this argument in a series of lectures, which will form the basis of a book, at a conference of economists, philosophers, and political scientists sponsored by the Liberty Fund, at Virginia Polytechnic Institute and State University, July 4–August 4, 1978.

Chapter 2

1. James Madison, *The Federalist* (New York: Modern Library, 1937), pp. 338–39.

2. Ibid., p. 337.

3. G. Warren Nutter, "Freedom in a Revolutionary Economy," in *The American Revolution: Three Views* (New York: American Brands, 1975), p. 119.

4. Roger A. Freeman, *The Growth of American Government* (Stanford: Hoover Institution Press, 1975), p. 1.

5. Thomas Borcherding, "One Hundred Years of Public Spending, 1870–1970," in Thomas Borcherding, ed., *Budgets and Bureaucrats: The Sources of Government Growth* (Durham, N.C.: Duke University Press, 1977), p. 32.

6. For more details, see Richard B. McKenzie, "Taxation and Redistribution," in Robert Formaini, ed., *Taxation and Society* (San Francisco: Cato Institute, 1981).

7. The "welfare tax" on many poor people exceeds 100 percent. For details on the size and consequences of the "welfare wall," see Martin Anderson, *Welfare: The Political Economy of Welfare Reform in the United States* (Stanford: Hoover Institution Press, 1978).

8. George Gilder, *Wealth and Poverty* (New York: Basic Books, 1981), p. 68.

9. James T. Bennett and Manuel H. Johnson, *The Political Economy of Federal Government Growth, 1959–1978* (College Station: Texas A&M University Press, 1980), pp. 31–32.

10. Ibid., p. 41.

11. Barbara Blumenthal, "Uncle Sam's Army of Invisible Employees," *National Journal*, May 5, 1979, pp. 730–33. Extrapolating from Blumenthal's estimate of half the departments, there may well be more than 14 million "invisible" employees working for the federal government. This means that in 1979 the federal government employed directly or indirectly almost 17 percent of all employed people.

12. Eugene McCarthy, *The Ultimate Tyranny: The Majority over the Majority* (New York: Harcourt Brace Jovanovich, 1980).

13. See Richard B. McKenzie and Robert J. Staaf, "Revenue Sharing and Monopoly Government," *Public Choice*, Fall 1978, pp. 93–97.

14. Walter B. Wriston, *Warning: The Law May Be Hazardous to Your Health* (New York: Citicorp, 1977), p. 3.

15. Researchers, for example, found that workers occasionally fall off wooden ladders that they make on construction sites. Hence, the Occupational Safety and Health Administration (OSHA) formulated very precise regulations on how these ladders must be built, specifying the minimum rung width and the angles of the side rails. For a review of other OSHA rules, see Robert Stewart Smith, *The Occupational Safety and Health Act: Its Goals and Its Achievements* (Washington, D.C.: American Enterprise Institute, 1976).

16. Paul W. MacAvoy, "The Rationale for Regulation of Gas Field Prices," and E. W. Kitch, "Regulation of the Field Market for Natural Gas by the Federal Power Commission," in Paul W. MacAvoy, ed., *The Crisis of the Regulatory Commissions* (New York: W. W. Norton & Co., 1970); Robert B. Helms, *Natural Gas Regulation: An Evaluation of FPC Controls* (Washington, D.C.: American Enterprise Institute, 1974); and J. Clayburn LaForce, *The Energy Crisis: The Moral Equivalent of Bamboozle* (Los Angeles: International Institute for Economic Research, 1978).

17. For surveys of the economic consequences of much modern regulation, see the publication list of organizations like the American Enterprise Institute, the Hoover Institution, and the Brookings Institution.

18. Murray L. Weidenbaum and Robert Defina, *The Cost of Federal Regulation of Economic Activity* (Washington, D.C.: American Enterprise Institute, 1978), p. 2.

19. James T. Bennett and Manuel H. Johnson, "The Political Economy of Federal Paperwork," *Policy Review*, Winter 1979, pp. 27–43.

20. Personal discussions with Bennett and Johnson.

21. Peter F. Drucker, "Coping with Those Extra Burdens," *Wall Street Journal*, May 2, 1979, p. 22.

22. Edward F. Denison, "Effects of Selected Changes in the Institutional and Human Environment upon Output per Unit of Input," *Survey of Current Business*, January 1978, pp. 21–24.

23. For more on the technical economic arguments for government protection (as well as counterarguments), see Richard B. McKenzie and Gordon Tullock, *Modern Political Economy* (New York: McGraw-Hill, 1978), chaps. 11–13.

24. Sam Peltzman, "The Effects of Automobile Safety Regulation," *Journal of Political Economy*, August 1975, pp. 677–725. Federally mandated "safety" changes in automobile manufacturing over the period 1968–1975 increased the average retail price of a 1976 passenger car by some $560 (Weidenbaum and Defina, *Cost of Federal Regulation*, pp. 13–15).

25. W. Mark Crain, *Automobile Safety: An Analysis of State Inspection*

(Washington, D.C.: American Enterprise Institute, 1980). Crain estimates that state inspection systems have increased automobile repair bills by 12 to 40 percent, depending on the state and inspection used. On average, repair bills have risen $90 per year per car because of inspection systems.

26. Colin D. Campbell, ed., *Wage-Price Controls in World War II, United States and Germany* (Washington, D.C.: American Enterprise Institute, 1971); Robert F. Lanzillotti, Mary T. Hamilton, and R. Blain Roberts, *Phase II in Review: The Price Commission Experience* (Washington, D.C.: Brookings Institution, 1975); and Marvin H. Kosters, *Controls and Inflation: The Economic Stabilization Program* (Washington, D.C.: American Enterprise Institute, 1975).

27. For a discussion of how direct and indirect government controls have affected prices of many goods, see Murray L. Weidenbaum, *Government-Mandated Price Increases: A Neglected Aspect of Inflation* (Washington, D.C.: American Enterprise Institute, 1975).

28. Elton Rayack, *Professional Power and the American Medical Association* (Cleveland: World Publishing Company, 1967); Rashi Fein, *The Doctor Shortage: An Economic Diagnosis* (Washington, D.C.: Brookings Institution, 1967); and Theodore Marmor, *The Politics of Medicare* (Chicago: Aldine Publishing Company, 1973).

29. Milton Friedman, *Capitalism and Freedom* (Chicago: University of Chicago Press, 1962), chap. 9; Benjamin Shimberg, et al., *Occupational Licensing: Practices and Policies* (Washington, D.C.: Public Affairs Press, 1973); "Restrictive Licensing of Dental Paraprofessionals," *Yale Law Review*, March 1974, pp. 806–26; U.S., Department of Health, Education, and Welfare, *State Licensing of Health Occupations*, Public Health Service Publication no. 2758 (Washington, D.C., 1967).

30. Sam Peltzman, *Regulation of Pharmaceutical Innovation: The 1961 Amendments* (Washington, D.C.: American Enterprise Institute, 1974); and William M. Wardell and Louis Lasagna, *Regulation and Drug Development* (Washington, D.C.: American Enterprise Institute, 1975).

31. William Wardell, "Therapeutic Implications of the Drug Lag," mimeo. (Rochester, N.Y.: University of Rochester Medical Center, 1973); as cited in Peltzman, *Regulation of Pharmaceutical Innovation* p. 89.

32. Wardell and Lasagna, *Regulation and Drug Development*, especially chap. 9; and Peltzman, *Regulation of Pharmaceutical Innovation*, chaps. 4–6.

33. Peltzman, *Regulation of Pharmaceutical Innovation*, p. 88.

34. Bruce Yandle, *Regulated Advertising and the Process of Self-Medication* (Washington, D.C.: Proprietary Association, 1978), pp. 7–8. Yan-

dle points out that "in the Antacid Monograph, the FDA approved the terms 'antacid,' 'heartburn,' 'acid indigestion' and 'sour stomach' for use in antacid labeling. No other terms could be used to describe the indications of use of an antacid. Under the FTC's proposed rule, it would be a civil offense for a manufacturer to tell consumers through advertising that the product is for 'relief of stomach misery due to excess stomach acid' or for 'relief of excess gastric acidity.' " (Ibid., p. 9.)

35. Bruce Yandle, "The Cost of Getting Nowhere at the FTC," *Regulation*, July/August 1981, pp. 43–47.

36. Arthur Andersen and Company, *Industry Briefs: Construction*, no. 77–5 (December 1, 1977), p. 9.

37. "Yak-Fat Story Illustrates Process: Agency's Role in Rail-Truck Fight Hit," *Washington Post*, January 18, 1965.

38. For elaborations on the basic theme, see George J. Stigler, *The Citizen and the State* (Chicago: University of Chicago Press, 1975). See also Almarin Phillips, ed., *Promoting Competition in Regulated Markets* (Washington, D.C.: Brookings Institution, 1975).

39. For a detailed account of the adverse effects of government efforts to regulate milk production in the "interest of protecting consumers" in one state, see William S. Rawson, *Public Regulation of Milk Prices: The South Carolina Experience* (Columbia: University of South Carolina, Bureau of Business and Economic Research, 1974). For an account of the political influence of the national dairy lobby, see Michael McMenamin and Walter McNamara, *Milking the Public: Political Scandals of the Dairy Lobby from LBJ to Jimmy Carter* (Chicago: Nelson-Hall, 1980).

40. William E. Simon, *A Time for Truth* (New York: McGraw-Hill, 1978), p. 73.

41. U.S., Council on Wage and Price Stability, *Catalogue of Federal Regulations Affecting the Iron and Steel Industry* (Washington, D.C., 1976), p. 216.

42. George J. Stigler, "The Theory of Regulation," *Bell Journal of Economics and Management Science*, Spring 1971, p. 3.

43. Research has found the obvious, that the efforts of people to influence government through campaign contributions rise exponentially with growth in government. Today, we have to be concerned with campaign contributions. One of the reasons campaign contributions are as high as they are is that government is as large as it is. See Mark Crain and Robert Tollison, "Some Monopoly Aspects of Politics" (Blacksburg: Virginia Polytechnic Institute and State University, Center for the Study of Public Choice, 1979).

Chapter 3

1. B. F. Skinner, *Science and Human Behavior* (New York: Macmillan, 1953), p. 447.

2. Tibor R. Machan, *The Pseudo-Science of B. F. Skinner* (New Rochelle, N.Y.: Arlington House Publishers, 1974), pp. 79–80.

3. Friedrich A. Hayek, *Individualism and Economic Order* (Chicago: University of Chicago Press, 1948), pp. 11–12.

4. Thomas Hobbes, *Leviathan*, C. B. MacPherson, ed. (Baltimore: Penguin Books, 1968), pp. 185–88.

5. John Locke, *The Second Treatise of Government*, Thomas P. Peardon, ed. (New York: Liberal Arts Press, 1954), pp. 32–33.

6. Harvard Professor John Rawls proposes that justice is the equivalent of fairness. Fairness is, in Rawls's theory, determined by the conditions under which the rules of social order are set. If the setting under which the social contract is developed is fair, then the social system and the consequences of that system are just. Rawls contends that just rules of social organization can emerge when people are conceptually placed behind a "veil of ignorance," that is, when they know nothing about their absolute or relative social position and, therefore, have no incentive to work for rules that will favor them. (John Rawls, *A Theory of Justice* [Cambridge, Mass.: Harvard University Press, 1971].) Although Hayek argues from a radically different conceptual framework, he takes much the same position on what constitutes just rules of conduct (F. A. Hayek, *Law, Legislation and Liberty*, vols. 1–2 [Chicago: University of Chicago Press, 1973, 1976]).

7. Karen I. Vaughn, "Economic Calculations Under Socialism: The Austrian Contribution," *Economic Inquiry*, October 1980, pp. 535–54.

8. John Kenneth Galbraith, *The New Industrial State* (New York: Houghton, Mifflin & Co., 1967).

9. Walter Lippmann, *Unto Caesar*; as cited in George H. Nash, *The Conservative Intellectual Movement in America Since 1945* (New York: Basic Books, 1979).

10. Hayek, *Individualism and Economic Order*, p. 32.

11. See Hayek, *Individualism and Economic Order*, idem, *The Constitution of Liberty* (Chicago: University of Chicago Press, 1960); and *The Road to Serfdom* (Chicago: University of Chicago Press, 1944).

12. Hayek, *The Constitution of Liberty*, p. 26.

13. For a more detailed discussion of how differences in preference and abilities of people can lead to trades, see Richard B. McKenzie and

Gordon Tullock, *Modern Political Economy* (New York: McGraw-Hill, 1978), chap. 5.

14. Adam Smith, *An Inquiry into the Nature and Causes of the Wealth of Nations* (New York: Modern Library, 1935).

15. Adam Smith, *The Theory of Moral Sentiments*, in Herbert W. Schneider, ed., *Adam Smith's Moral and Political Philosophy*, (New York: Harper & Row, 1970), p. 275.

16. Stewart Macaulay, "Elegant Models, Empirical Pictures, and the Complexities of Contracts," *Law and Society Review*, Winter 1977, pp. 507–8. See also Stewart Macaulay, "Non-Contractual Relations in Business: A Preliminary Study," *American Sociological Review*, February 1963, pp. 55–67.

17. Frank H. Knight, "The Limits of Economics as a Science," in *The Ethics of Competition* (Chicago: University of Chicago Press, 1976), pp. 105–47.

18. Frank H. Knight, "Freedom as Fact and Criterion," in *Freedom and Reform: Essays in Economics and Social Philosophy* (New York: Harper and Row, 1947), pp. 13–14.

Chapter 4

1. As related by my colleague Hugh Macaulay.

2. Adam Smith, *The Theory of Moral Sentiments* (Indianapolis, Ind.: Liberty Classics, 1976), pp. 380–81.

3. George C. Lodge, *The New American Ideology* (New York: Alfred A. Knopf, 1975), p. 34.

4. Lutheran Church of America, "A Cry of Injustice and an Ethic of Response" (March 20, 1979, preliminary draft).

5. See Richard B. Mancke, "Competition in the Oil Industry," in Edward J. Mitchell, ed., *Vertical Integration in the Oil Industry* (Washington, D.C.: American Enterprise Institute, 1976), pp. 35–72.

6. There is the frequently heard argument that coupons need to be distributed so the poor can have gasoline. That is a smoke screen. The poor are generally not the ones who do all the driving; the really poor do not have cars and, generally, would not receive coupons.

7. George F. Will, "Coupon Rationing: A Messy Proposal, *Greenville News*, June 21, 1979, p. 4-A.

8. John Stuart Mill, *On Liberty*, in Marshall Cohen, ed., *The Philosophy of J.S. Mill* (New York: Modern Library, 1961), pp. 190–92.

Chapter 5

1. "The Travels and Adventures of Three Princes of Serendip: The Tale of the Princes," as translated from Persian to French and then to English and found in J. Wallace Hamilton, *Serendipity* (Westwood, N.J.: Flemming H. Revell Co., 1965), p. 9. See also Elizabeth Jamison Hodges, *The Three Princes of Serendip* (New York: Atheneum, 1966).

2. See Hamilton, *Serendipity*, pp. 17–25. James H. Austin, *Chase, Chance, and Creativity: The Lucky Art of Novelty* (New York: Columbia University Press, 1978), includes discussions of many serendipities in science.

3. Hamilton, *Serendipity*, p. 24.

4. Marx wrote in *Capital*, "The bourgeoisie and the capitalistic system they control, during its rule of scarce one hundred years, has created more massive and more colossal productive forces than have all preceding generations together. Subjection of Nature's forces to man, machinery, and application of chemistry to industry and agriculture, steam navigation, railways, electric telegraphs, clearing of whole continents for cultivation, canalization of rivers, whole populations conjured out of the ground—what earlier century had even a presentiment that such productive forces slumbered in the lap of the social labor?" (Quoted in M. M. Bober, *Karl Marx's Interpretation of History* [New York: W. W. Norton & Co., 1965], pp. 18–19.) In order to attain the communist ideal of "giving according to need," a tremendously productive economy is required, according to Marx; hence, capitalism is a necessary stage of economic development before the communist utopia could be reached.

5. Thomas Hobbes, *Leviathan*, C. B. MacPherson, ed. (Baltimore: Penguin Books, 1968), especially pp. 185–88.

6. Armen A. Alchian and Harold Demsetz, "The Property Rights Paradigm," *Journal of Economic History*, March 1973, p. 17.

7. James M. Buchanan, *The Limits of Liberty: Between Anarchy and Leviathan* (Chicago: University of Chicago Press, 1975), p. 9.

8. There is actually nothing in free enterprise economics that prevents one family from renting a lawn mower to another family, thus increasing the utilization of the lawn mower. In a free enterprise system people are *free* to strike whatever deal they wish with others.

9. Taken from Richard B. McKenzie and Gordon Tullock, *The New World of Economics: Explorations into Human Behavior*, rev. ed. (Homewood, Ill.: Richard D. Irwin, 1978), pp. 32–35.

10. Beginning in the 1960s, the government began to assert its right of ownership to airspace and waterways, thus converting the resources in

some areas from communal ownership to state ownership, an improvement in some but not all instances. For a detailed discussion of the "logic of pollution," see Hugh H. Macaulay and T. Bruce Yandle, *Environmental Use and the Market* (New York: Lexington Books, 1977).

11. See Rodgers Taylor Denne, "From Common to Private Property: The Enclosure of the Open Range" (Ph.D. diss., University of Washington, 1975).

12. Private ownership of whales, it must be admitted, is made difficult by their annual migration, which can cover as much as 6,000 miles of ocean and makes fencing them in like cattle difficult, to say the least.

13. Paul A. Samuelson, *Economics: An Introductory Analysis*, 3rd ed. (New York: McGraw-Hill, 1955), pp. 271–72.

14. Gordon Tullock, *The Vote Motive* (London: Institute of Economic Affairs, 1976), p. 10.

15. Donald S. Stokes and Warren E. Miller, "Party Government and the Saliency of Congress," *Public Opinion Quarterly*, Winter 1962, pp. 531–46.

16. Richard B. McKenzie, *The Political Economy of the Education Process* (Boston: Martinus Niejhoff, 1979), chap. 10.

17. Think of how little time a person would spend looking for an automobile if he knew the car he gets is ultimately determined by majority vote of the people in his community or state.

18. Kenneth J. Arrow, *Social Choice and Individual Values* (New York: John Wiley & Sons, 1963).

19. Gordon Tullock, *Toward a Mathematics of Politics* (Ann Arbor: University of Michican Press, 1967), chap. 3.

20. For a detailed analysis of how the needs of politics influence economic policy and how economic theory affects the policy recommendations of politicians, see Edward R. Tufte, *Political Control of the Economy* (Princeton, N.J.: Princeton University Press, 1978).

21. Jack Anderson, "Washington Merry-Go-Round," *Raleigh News and Observer*, July 15, 1974.

22. F. A. Hayek, *The Constitution of Liberty* (Chicago: University of Chicago Press, 1960), p. 16.

23. Frank H. Knight, "Intellectual Confusion on Morals and Economics," *International Journal of Ethics* (January 1935); quoted in Buchanan, *The Limits of Liberty*, p. vi.

24. Adam Smith, *An Inquiry into the Nature and Causes of the Wealth of Nations* (New York: Modern Liberty, 1935), p. 250.

25. See "How to Slow the Rate of Inflation" (General Motors advertisement), *Newsweek*, April 23, 1979; and "Down with Big Business" (editorial), *Wall Street Journal*, April 18, 1979, p. 24.

26. Charles G. Koch, in a public letter from the Council for a Competitive/Economy (1979), pp. 1–2.

27. Ibid., p. 2.

28. Ibid.

29. See Friedrich A. Hayek, *The Road to Serfdom* (Chicago: University of Chicago Press, 1944).

Chapter 6

1. Jonathan R. T. Hughes, *The Governmental Habit: Economic Controls from Colonial Times to the Present* (New York: Basic Books, 1977).

2. John Maynard Keynes, *The General Theory of Employment, Interest, and Money* (New York: Harcourt, Brace, & World, 1936), p. 383.

3. Many economists dispute this contention. They argue that federal deficits mean the government is borrowing funds that would have been borrowed by private investors. The relevant question is whether and to what extent is a dollar of government demand offset by a dollar reduction in private investment demand. Monetarists argue that there is a complete offsetting effect. Keynes essentially argued that government deficit spending uses loanable funds that would not otherwise have been used and increases the velocity of money.

4. James M. Buchanan and Richard E. Wagner, *Democracy in Deficit: The Political Legacy of Lord Keynes* (New York: Academic Press, 1977).

5. Much of President Carter's interest in price guidelines was to shift the blame through the media from the public to the private sector.

6. Richard A. Ippolito, "The Effects of Price Regulation in the Automobile Insurance Industry," *Journal of Law and Economics* 22, no. 1 (April 1979): 55–90.

7. For a discussion of the disproportionate political influence of special interest groups, see Anthony Downs, *An Economic Theory of Democracy* (New York: Harper & Row, 1957); Gordon Tullock, *Toward a Mathematics of Politics* (Ann Arbor: University of Michigan Press, 1967); and Mancur Olson, *The Logic of Collective Action* (Cambridge, Mass.: Harvard University Press, 1967).

Chapter 7

1. "Sixth Amendment Open Trial Guarantee Benefit Accused, Not Press of Public," *United States Law Week*, July 3, 1979, p. 1001.

2. "First Amendment," *United States Law Week*, January 2, 1979, p. 3440.

3. Myron Farber, reporter for the *New York Times* and a defendant in a similar but earlier trial, announced in his defense that "the issue here is the right of an unfettered press to keep the country informed . . . What I am trying to do is uphold the Constitution of the United States." (Quoted in William P. Cheshire, "The Imperial Press," *National Review*, August 17, 1979, p. 1020.)

4. *Newsweek*, July 16, 1979, p. 60.

5. James J. Kilpatrick, "Ruling Didn't Imperil Freedom," Greenville *News*, July 9, 1981, p. 10.

6. Cheshire, "The Imperial Press," p. 1020.

7. Walter B. Wriston, "Repressing Economic News, *Wall Street Journal*, May 4, 1979, editorial page.

8. "The Great American Bureaucratic Propaganda Machine," *U.S. News & World Report*, August 27, 1979, p. 43.

9. Ibid., pp. 44–45.

10. Ibid., p. 47.

11. Ronald Coase, "The Market for Goods and the Market for Ideas," *American Economic Review*, papers and proceedings, May 1974, p. 389.

12. Alexander Hamilton, *The Federalist* (New York: Modern Library, 1937), p. 559.

Chapter 8

1. From personal conversations.

2. For an example of a movement to limit one state's expenditures, see F. Jerry Ingram and Michael Maloney, "Limiting State Government Expenditures in South Carolina: An Analysis of the Proposal of the South Carolina Committee for Tax and Spending Limitations," mimeo. (Columbia: South Carolina Committee for Tax and Spending Limitations, 1979). See also George Uhimchuk, "Constitutional Tax Limits at the State Level: An Overview and Selected Case Studies" (Ph.D. diss. [Blacksburg: Virginia Polytechnic Institute and State University, Center for the Study of Public

Choice, 1980]), especially chaps. 1–3; and Geoffrey Brennan and James M. Buchanan, *The Power to Tax: The Analytical Foundations of a Fiscal Constitution* (Cambridge, Eng.: Cambridge University Press, 1980).

3. Most people understand that waste abounds in government and that government can be made to be more scrupulous in its expenditures. An abrupt movement to a smaller federal government would be politically impossible as well as economically disruptive. To move gradually to smaller government (as a percentage of income), growth in government revenues can be made some fraction (say, 50 percent) of the *growth* in personal income until the desired percentage size of government is achieved. Such a provision will ensure that even as government revenues grow to some extent, the *relative* size of government will fall gradually and predictably.

4. James M. Buchanan and Richard E. Wagner, *Democracy in Deficit: The Political Legacy of Lord Keynes* (New York: Academic Press, 1977).

5. James M. Buchanan and Gordon Tullock, *The Calculus of Consent: The Constitutional Foundations of Democracy* (Ann Arbor: University of Michigan Press, 1962).

6. Alternatively, the federal government utilizes deficit spending, which is then financed directly or indirectly by newly created money. The federal government's demand for loanable funds drives up the rate of interest, which has frequently in the past brought the Federal Reserve into the market as a buyer of government bonds. The net effect is still an increase in the money supply due, albeit indirectly, to deficit spending.

7. Milton Friedman and Rose Friedman, *Free to Choose: A Personal Statement* (New York: Harcourt Brace Jovanovich, 1980), especially chap. 9; and Milton Friedman, *Dollars and Deficits* (Englewood Cliffs, N.J.: Prentice-Hall, 1968), chap. 1.

8. F. A. Hayek, *Denationalization of Money*, 2d ed. (London: Institute of Economic Affairs, 1978); and idem, *Law, Legislation, and Liberty*, vol. 3 (Chicago: University of Chicago Press, 1979), chap. 14. See also Geoffrey Brennan and James M. Buchanan, *Monopoly in Money and Inflation: The Case for a Constitution to Discipline Government* (London: Institute of Economic Affairs, 1981).

9. The estimate of regulatory costs could be made by an independent agency such as the National Bureau of Economic Research.

10. Not all day-to-day political problems can be resolved by constitutional means, and the accomplishment of such a goal should not be attempted. Even with tax and regulatory limitations, political factions will continue to wrestle with the problem of who actually bears the cost of

government, the people who pay taxes or the people who bear the cost of government regulations.

11. See, in particular, George J. Stigler, "The Theory of Economic Regulation," *Bell Journal of Economics and Management Science*, Spring 1978, pp. 3–21. See also, the publication lists of the American Enterprise Institute for Public Policy Research, the Brookings Institution, and the Institute for Economic Affairs. For a short review of many studies, see Paul W. MacAvoy, *The Regulated Industries and the Economy* (New York: W. W. Norton & Co., 1979).

12. For a detailed account of the arguments that follow, see Richard B. McKenzie, "A Constitutional Perspective for the Deregulation Movement," (Clemson, S.C.: Clemson University, Department of Economics, 1979 [working paper]).

13. The "windfall profits tax," passed by Congress in 1980, along with legislation to deregulate the oil industry by the early 1980s is an example of the tax-compensation scheme mentioned here. For details on the argument, see Richard B. McKenzie and Gordon Tullock, *The New World of Economics: Explorations into the Human Experience*, 3rd ed. (Homewood, Ill.: Richard D. Irwin, 1981), pp. 221–25.

14. George J. Stigler, "Elementary Economic Education," *American Economic Review*, 53 (May 1963): 653–59.

15. Richard B. McKenzie, *The Political Economy of the Educational Process* (Boston: Martinus Nijhoff Publishing, 1979), especially chap. 9; and idem, "Where is the Economics in Economic Education?" *Journal of Economic Education*, Fall 1977, pp. 5–13.

16. For a thorough review of economic education studies undertaken over the past twenty years, see John J. Siegfried and Rendigs Fels, "Teaching College Economics: A Survey," *Journal of Economic Literature*, September 1979, pp. 923–69.

17. Tom Bethell, "TV, Inflation, and Government Handouts," *Wall Street Journal*, July 8, 1980, editorial page.

18. The public goods argument for economic education has been evaluated by the author on several occasions. The theoretical and empirical arguments are summarized in *The Political Economy of the Educational Process*, chap. 9. See also Richard B. McKenzie, "Principles of Political Economy in Principles of Economics," Jeff Clark, ed., *Innovations in Principles of Economics* (New York: Joint Council on Economic Education, 1979).

19. Anne Wortham, "A Black Writer's View of *Roots*," *Reason*, May 1977, p. 25.

Bibliography

Anderson, Martin. *Welfare: The Political Economy of Welfare Reform in the United States*. Stanford: Hoover Institution Press, 1978.

Anderson, Terry L., and Hill, Peter J. *The Birth of a Transfer Society*. Stanford: Hoover Institution Press, 1980.

Arrow, Kenneth J. *Social Choice and Individual Values*. New York: John Wiley & Son, 1963.

Bennett, James T., and Johnson, Manuel H. *The Political Economy of Federal Government Growth, 1959–1968*. College Station: Texas A&M University Press, 1980.

———— and ————. "The Political Economy of Federal Paperwork." *Policy Review*, Winter 1979, pp. 27–43.

Berger, Raoul. *Government by Judiciary: The Transformation of the Fourteenth Amendment*. Cambridge, Mass.: Harvard University Press, 1977.

Bethell, Tom. "TV, Inflation, and Government Handouts." *Wall Street Journal*, July 8, 1980, editorial page.

Borcherding, Thomas E. "One Hundred Years of Public Spending, 1870–1970." In Thomas Borcherding, ed., *Budgets and Bureaucrats: The Source of Government*. Durham, N.C.: Duke University Press, 1977.

Brennan, Geoffrey, and Buchanan, James M. *Monopoly in Money and Inflation: The Case for a Constitution to Discipline Government*. London: Institute of Economic Affairs, 1981.

———— and ————. *The Power to Tax: The Analytical Foundations of a Fiscal Constitution*. Cambridge, Eng.: Cambridge University Press, 1981.

Buchanan, James M. *The Limits of Liberty: Between Anarchy and Leviathan*. Chicago: University of Chicago Press, 1975.

————, and Tullock, Gordon. *The Calculus of Consent: The Constitutional Foundations of Democracy*. Ann Arbor: University of Michigan Press, 1962.

————, and Wagner, Richard E. *Democracy in Deficit: The Political Legacy of Lord Keynes*. New York: Academic Press, 1977.

Campbell, Colin D., ed. *Wage-Price Controls in World War II, United States and Germany*. Washington, D.C.: American Enterprise Institute, 1971.

Coase, Ronald."The Market for Goods and the Market for Ideas." *American Economic Review*, papers and proceedings, May 1974, pp. 384–91.

Crain, W. Mark. *Automobile Safety: An Analysis of State Inspection*. Washington, D.C.: American Enterprise Institute, 1980.

Denison, Edward F. "Effects of Selected Changes in the Institutional and Human Environment upon Output Per Unit of Input." *Survey of Current Business*, January 1978, pp. 21–24.

Denne, Rodgers Taylor. "From Common to Private Property: The Enclosure of the Open Range." Ph.D. diss., University of Washington, 1975.

Downs, Anthony. *An Economic Theory of Democracy*. New York: Harper & Row, 1957.

Fein, Rashi. *The Doctor Shortage: An Economic Diagnosis*. Washington, D.C.: Brookings Institution, 1967.

Freeman, Roger A. *The Growth of American Government*. Stanford: Hoover Institution Press, 1975.

Friedman, Milton. *Capitalism and Freedom*. Chicago: University of Chicago Press, 1962.

————. *Dollars and Deficits*. Englewood Cliffs, N.J.: Prentice-Hall, 1968.

————. *An Economist's Protest: Columns in Political Economy*. Glen Ridge, N.J.: Thomas Horton & Daughters, 1972.

————, and Friedman, Rose. *Free to Choose: A Personal Statement*. New York: Harcourt Brace Jovanovich, 1980.

Gilder, George. *Wealth and Poverty*. New York: Basic Books, 1981.

Hayek, Friedrich A. *The Constitution of Liberty*. Chicago: University of Chicago Press, 1960.

————. *Denationalization of Money*, 2d ed. London: Institute of Economic Affairs, 1978.

————. *Individualism and Economic Order*. Chicago: University of Chicago Press, 1948.

————. *Law, Legislation, and Liberty*. 3 vols. Chicago: University of Chicago Press, 1973, 1976, 1979.

————. *The Road to Serfdom*. Chicago: University of Chicago Press, 1944.

Helms, Robert B. *Natural Gas Regulation: An Evaluation of PPC Controls.* Washington, D.C.: American Enterprise Institute, 1974.

Hobbes, Thomas. *Leviathan*, C. B. MacPherson, ed. Baltimore: Penguin Books, 1968.

Hughes, Jonathan R. T. *The Governmental Habit: Economic Controls From Colonial Times to the Present.* New York: Basic Books, 1977.

Ingram, F. Jerry, and Maloney, Michael. "Limiting State Government Expenditures in South Carolina: An Analysis of the Proposal of the South Carolina Committee for Tax and Spending Limitations." Mimeographed. Columbia: South Carolina Committee for Tax and Spending Limitations, 1979.

Knight, Frank H. "Freedom as Fact and Criterion." In *Freedom and Reform: Essays in Economics and Social Philosophy*. New York: Harper and Row, 1947.

———. "The Limits of Economics as a Science." In *The Ethics of Competition*. Chicago: University of Chicago Press, 1976.

Kosters, Marvin H. *Controls and Inflation: The Economic Stabilization Program.* Washington, D.C.: American Enterprise Institute, 1975.

LaForce, J. Clayburn. *The Energy Crisis: The Moral Equivalent of Bamboozle.* Los Angeles: International Institute for Economic Research, 1978.

Lanzillotti, Robert F.; Hamilton, Mary T.; and Roberts, R. Blain. *Phase II in Review: The Price Commission Experience.* Washington, D.C.: Brookings Institution, 1975.

Locke, John. *The Second Treatise of Government.* Thomas P. Peardon, ed. New York: Liberal Arts Press, 1954.

Lodge, George C. *The New American Ideology.* New York: Alfred A. Knopf, 1975.

Macaulay, Hugh H., and Yandle, T. Bruce. *Environmental Use and the Market.* New York: Lexington Books, 1977.

McCarthy, Eugene. *The Ultimate Tyranny: The Majority Over the Majority.* New York: Harcourt Brace Jovanovich, 1980.

MacAvoy, Paul W., ed. *The Crisis of the Regulatory Commissions.* New York: W. W. Norton & Co., 1970.

Machan, Tibor R. *The Pseudo-Science of B. F. Skinner.* New Rochelle, N.Y.: Arlington House Publishers, 1974.

McKenzie, Richard B. *The Political Economy of the Educational Process.* Boston: Martinus Nijhoff, Publishing, 1979

————. "Principles of Political Economy in Principles of Economics." In Jeff Clark, ed., *Innovations in Principles of Economics*. New York: Joint Council on Economic Education, 1979.

————. "Where is the Economics in Economic Education?" *Journal of Economic Education*, Fall 1977, pp. 5–13.

————, and Staaf, Robert J. "Revenue Sharing and Monopoly Government." *Public Choice*, Fall 1978, pp. 93–97.

————, and Tullock, Gordon. *Modern Political Economy*. New York: McGraw-Hill, 1978.

————, and Tullock, Gordon. *The New World of Economics: Explorations into the Human Experience*, rev. ed. Homewood, Ill.: Richard D. Irwin, 1981.

McMenamin, Michael, and McNamara, Walter. *Milking the Public: Political Scandals of the Dairy Lobby from LBJ to Jimmy Carter*. Chicago: Nelson-Hall, 1980.

Madison, James. *The Federalist*. New York: Modern Library, 1937.

Mancke, Richard B. "Competition in the Oil Industry." In Edward J. Mitchell, ed., *Vertical Integration in the Oil Industry*. Washington, D.C.: American Enterprise Institute, 1976.

Marmor, Theodore. *The Politics of Medicare*. Chicago: Aldine, 1973.

Mill, John Stuart. *On Liberty*. In Marshall Cohen, ed., *Philosophy of J. S. Mill*. New York: Modern Library, 1961.

Miller, James C., and Yandle, T. Bruce, eds. *Benefit-Cost Analysis of Social Regulation Case Studies from the Council on Wage and Price Stability*. Washington, D.C.: American Enterprise Institute, 1979.

Nutter, G. Warren. "Freedom in a Revolutionary Economy." In *The American Revolution: Three Views*. New York: American Brands, 1975.

Olson, Mancur. *The Logic of Collective Action*. Cambridge, Mass.: Harvard University Press, 1967.

Peltzman, Sam. "The Effects of Automobile Safety Regulation." *Journal of Political Economy*, August 1975, pp. 677–725.

————. *Regulation of Pharmaceutical Innovation: The 1961 Amendments*. Washington, D.C.: American Enterprise Institute, 1974.

Phillips, Almarin, ed. *Promoting Competition in Regulated Markets*. Washington, D.C.: Brookings Institution, 1975.

Rawls, John. *A Theory of Justice*. Cambridge, Mass.: Harvard University Press, 1971.

Rawson, William S. *Public Regulation of Milk Prices: The South Carolina Experience.* Columbia: University of South Carolina, Bureau of Business and Economic Research, 1974.

Rayack, Elton. *Professional Power and the American Medicine: The Economics of the American Medical Association.* Cleveland: World Publishing Co., 1967.

Ropke, Wilhelm. *A Humane Economy: The Social Framework of the Free Market.* South Bend, Ind.: Gateway, 1960.

Siegan, Bernard H. *Economic Liberties and the Constitution.* Chicago: University of Chicago Press, 1981.

Siegfried, John J., and Rendigs, Fels. "Teaching College Economics: A Survey." *Journal of Economic Literature*, September 1979, pp. 923–69.

Simon, William E. *A Time for Truth.* New York: McGraw-Hill, 1978.

Smith, Adam. *An Inquiry into the Nature and Causes of the Wealth of Nations.* New York: Modern Library, 1935.

———. *The Theory of Moral Sentiments.* In Herbert W. Schneider, ed., *Adam Smith's Moral and Political Philosophy.* New York: Harper & Row, 1970.

Stigler, George J. *The Citizen and the State.* Chicago: University of Chicago Press, 1975.

———. "Elementary Economic Education." *American Economic Review*, 53 (May 1963): 653–59.

———. "The Theory of Economic Regulation." *Bell Journal of Economics and Management*, Spring 1970, pp. 3–21.

Tufte, Edward R. *Political Control of the Economy.* Princeton, N.J.: Princeton University Press, 1978.

Tullock, Gordon. *Toward a Mathematics of Politics.* Ann Arbor: University of Michigan Press, 1967.

———. *The Vote Motive.* London: Institute of Economic Affairs, 1976.

Uhimchuk, George A. "Constitutional Tax Limits at the State Level: An Overview and Selected Case Studies." Ph.D. diss. Virginia Polytechnic Institute and State University, Center for the Study of Public Choice, 1980.

Vaughn, Karen I. "Economic Calculations Under Socialism: The Austrian Calculation." *Economic Inquiry*, October 1980, pp. 535–54.

Wardell, William M., and Lasagna, Louis. *Regulation and Drug Development.* Washington, D.C.: American Enterprise Institute, 1975.

Weidenbaum, Murray L. *Government-Mandated Price Increases: A Neglected Aspect of Inflation*. Washington, D.C.: American Enterprise Institute, 1975.

————, and Defina, Robert. *The Cost of Federal Regulation of Economic Activity*. Washington, D.C.: American Enterprise Institute, 1978.

Wriston, Walter B. *Warning: The Law May Be Hazardous to Your Health*. New York: Citicorp, 1977.

Yandle, Bruce. *Regulated Advertising and the Process of Self-Medication*. Washington, D.C.: Proprietary Association, 1978.

Index

A

Adams, Brock, 35, 86
Agee, Philip, 144
Agriculture, 86, 132–33
Alchain, Armen, 99
Authority, 10–11, 76
Automobile, 35; insurance, 131–32
Auxiliary precautions, 15, 114, 128, 162–63

B

Balanced budget norm, 127, 164
Banks, 36–37
Behavior, 50; model, 67; restrictions, 98. *See also* Skinner, B.F.
Bennett, James, 19, 28
Berger, Raoul, 7–8
Bergland, Bob, 39–40
Bill of Rights, 115, 151
Birthrate, 137, 138
Borcherding, Thomas, 17, 18
Brown, Jerry, 75
Buchanan, James: constitutional anarchy, 8; agreement, 94, 100; property, 99; balanced budget norm, 127, 164; voting majority, 165

Budget: federal, 17, 19, 20; state and local, 20, 23–24; government, 28; public, 43
Budgetary deficit, 126
Budgetary dependence, 23–24
Budgets and externalities, 137–38
Building codes, 134
Bureaucratic control, 113–14
Business, 26–28, 41–43, 66, 121–22, 145
Businessmen, 9, 118–22
Buyers, 83, 84

C

Carter, Jimmy, 25, 61, 76, 86–87, 145, 151
Carter administration, 144
Cash grants, 135
Censorship, 151–52
Centralization of government, 25
Centralization of power, 23
Cheshire, William, 150
Coase, Ronald, 153
Codes: tax, 21; building, 134
Coercion, 22, 52, 81–82, 91, 150
Collective decisions, 15, 22, 57, 91, 106

Collective institutions, 21
Collectivism, 77
Collectivist movement, 78. *See also*
  Social values
Collectivists, 87, 88, 90, 105, 118–
  19
Collectivization: of charity, 70; of
  economic activity, 58. *See also*
  Organizational structure
Commission on Federal Paperwork,
  152
Committee for Economic Develop-
  ment, 3–4
Common interest, *see* Social Values
Communal property, 101–4, 133,
  134
Communication, 10
Communitarianism, 77
Competition, 24, 63, 89; of ideas,
  149
Competitive ideas, 148–49
Compound republic, 24
Computers, 59–60
Congress, 42, 75–76, 82–83
Constituency, 22, 23
Constitution, 10, 115, 116–17;
  U.S., 13, 143–45, 156, 172; of
  freedom, 115
Constitutional anarchy, 6, 8
Constitutional constraints on gov-
  ernment, 1, 7, 9–11, 125. *See also*
  Free economy
Constitutional government, 9–11
Constitutional limitations, 13
Consumer goods, 16
Consumer protection, 29–40
Consumer wants and needs, 59–60
Contracts, social, 50, 65–66, 160,
  180
Controls: mercantilist, 2, 15; price,
  36, 89; production, 133

Corruption, 23
Costs: 32–34, 55, 131, 166; production, 26; compliance, 28; spillover, 129–35 *passim;* external,
  129–40 *passim. See also* Externalities
Coupons, rationing, 89, 90
Crain, W. Mark, 35
Crime, 133

D

Demand, 21, 23
Decisions: collective, 15, 22, 57,
  91, 106; private, 21, 22, 57
Deficiencies of democracy: 104; de-
  cisions by majority, 105–6; deci-
  sions determined by median vot-
  ers, 106–7; political ignorance,
  108–9; special interest groups,
  110; voting inconsistencies, 110–
  11; political expediency, 111–13;
  bureaucratic control, 113–14
Democracy, 7, 8, 21–22, 56, 91,
  104–14
Demsetz, Harold, 99
Denison, Edward F., 29
Denver, John, 135–38
Department of Energy, 75–76, 84,
  152
Department of Housing and Urban
  Development, 39
Deregulation, 167–68
Disaster relief, 134
Distribution: wealth, 69–70; in-
  comes, 77; property, 100
Diversity, 45, 47
Drucker, Peter, 28–29
Drug regulations, 37–39. *See also*
  Food and Drug Administration

E

Earthquakes, 134
Economic education, 3–5, 169–72
Economic theory, 130
Education, 135
Efficiency, economic, 135
Efficiency: production, 64; governmental, 129–30, 135
Einstein, Albert, 142
Employment: federal, 18–19; state and local, 20
Employment Act of 1946, 82–83
Energy, 83–84; crisis, 84–90, 92–93; conservation, 87; prices, 87
Entrepreneurs, 117–18
Environment, 130
Equality before the law, 47–54 *passim*, 90–91, 121, 160
Equality of men, 51, 52
Ethical code, 65
Expansion, 57–58. *See also* Government expansion
External costs, *see* Costs, Externalities
Externalities, 130, 137–40

F

Farm markets, 133
Federal government: expenditures, 6, 15–18; expansion, 6, 15–25, 40–44, 127, 139–40; receipts, 16; budget, 17, 19, 20; employment, 18–21; regulation, 25–29, 128–30, 132–35, 145; intervention, 34–40, 84–90, 105, 130, 133, 145

Federal Register, 26, 27
Federal republic, 13, 14
Federal Reserve, 127
Federal Trade Commission, 38–39
Fire protection, 133, 134
First Amendment, 143–54 *passim*, 162; Rights, 148–49
Fiscal constitution, 164
Fiscal irresponsibility, 127
Fiscal policy, 126–27
Floods, 134
Food and Drug Administration, 33–38 *passim*
Food stamps, 133, 135
Forced riders, 71
Founding Fathers, 12, 13–15, 144, 154, 156, 162–63
Frankfurter, Felix, 10
"Free at last," 2
Freedom, 46, 48–50, 68, 82, 172; unlimited, 98; of speech, 145–51; of press, 147, 151, 154; of religion, 148, 151. *See also* Individual freedom
Free economy, 161–68. *See also* Free market
Free enterprise, *see* Free market
Freeman, Roger A., 17
Free market, 2, 7, 8, 9, 14, 63, 93; opposition 43–44, 54, 56, 60, 64–71, 97; self-destruction, 116–17; and private property, 116–18; and businessmen, 118–22; and competitive ideas, 148–49, 153; conclusions, 154–56. *See also* Federal government, Freedom
Free-rider, 71; problem, 173
Free society, 115–16
Free trade, 62–69 *passim*
Friedman, Milton, 124–25, 165, 178

G

Galbraith, John Kenneth, 58
Gannett Company, Inc. v. *DePasquale*,
    143
Gilder, George, 18
Government: expansion of state and
    local, 20–21; large, 23, 24, 42,
    114, 138, 150, 152; small, 23–25,
    43, 137; centralization of, 25; un-
    restricted, 33, 117–22 *passim*; lim-
    ited, 92, 126. *See also* Federal
    Government, State government
Government regulation, *see* Federal
    government
Governmental habit, 123
Grants: state, 23; federal, 23–24;
    cash, 135

H

Haley, Alex, 173
Hamilton, Alexander, 154–55
Hamilton, J. Wallace, 95–97
Harrod, Roy, 128
Hayek, Friedrich: freedom, 46, 48,
    115–16; individualism, 50–51,
    58–59; markets, 60; monetary re-
    form, 165
Hitler, Adolf, 79, 148
Hobbes, Thomas, 10, 52–53, 99,
    118
Hughes, Jonathan R. T., 125
Human capital, 135
Human rights, 145
Humphrey, Hubert, 83

I

Iacocca, Lee, 121–22
Ideas: in goods, 147; in print and
    speech, 147; competitive, 148–49

Ignorance, political, 108–9
Income, national, 17, 18
Income taxes, 26, 163
Individual freedom, 2; and the free
    market, 14, 54–60, 64–72, 137;
    and private decision making, 21–
    22; and social regulation, 25; and
    free trade, 62–64; and private
    property, 100–4, 116; effects of
    unrestricted government, 117–18
Individualism, 51, 58, 59, 77-70
Individuality, 45, 47
Industry, 25, 26, 36, 39, 42
Inefficiency, 21, 139. *See also* Fed-
    eral government
Inflation, 29, 112, 127–28
Insurance, 131–32, 137
Interest, multiplicity of, 14
Interstate Commerce Commission
    (ICC), 39
Ippolito, Richard A., 131
Iran, 84

J

Jefferson, Thomas, 1, 2
Johnson, Manuel H., 19, 28
Jones, Jim, 148, 153
Justice, 51

K

Kennedy administration, 113, 127
Keynes, John Maynard, 96, 125,
    128, 140, 184
Keynesian economics, 127, 129
Kilpatrick, James, 144
King, Martin Luther, 2, 3
Knight, Frank, 55, 67, 116, 160
Koch, Charles, 119–20, 122
Kraft, Joseph, 152

L

Large government, 23, 24, 42, 114, 138, 150, 152. See also Federal Government
Law, 10–11, 13, 42, 51–53
Leadership, 172
Legal system, 42, 65
Limited government, 92, 126
Lincoln, Abraham, 47–48, 51, 52
Lippman, Walter, 58
Local government, 20–21, 23–24
Locke, John, 53
Lodge, George C., 77
Lutheran Church of America, 80, 81

M

Macaulay, Stewart, 65–66, 156, 162
Machan, Tibor, 49
Madison, James, 13–15, 114–15
Majority rule, 13, 14, 22, 90, 105–6, 125
Management, 28–29
Manne, Henry, 170
Market: competitive, 43, 62–64, 83–84; investment, 43; exchanges, 54–60; failures, 105, controls, 151; inefficiencies, 167. See also Free market
Marx, Karl, 66, 97, 182
McCarthy, Eugene, 22, 176
Median voters, 106–7
Mill, John Stuart, 22, 48, 91, 181
Mine and thine, 53, 97, 99, 104
Minimal state, 135–38
Minimum wage, 145
Monetary limitations, 165–66
Money supply, 127

Monopoly power, 24, 35, 88, 90, 105, 149
Moral behavior, 65, 66
Morality, 8–11
Moral significance of the individual, 48–51
Multiplicity of interest, 14

N

Nader, Ralph, 34
National defense, 104
National health insurance, 137
National interest, 24
Natural gas, 26
New York Times, 144
Ninth Amendment, 151
Nixon administration, 36
Nutter, G. Warren, 12, 44

O

Occupational Safety and Health Administration, 26, 27–28, 177
Oil: companies, 66; shortage, 75, 84. *See also under* Energy
Organization of Petroleum Exporting Countries, 24
Organizational structures, 57, 58, 78. *See also* Small groups
Ortega y Gasset, Jose, 53

P

Peltzman, Sam, 38
Pennington v. *Kansas*, 143
Police protection, 133–34

Political competition, 106
Political investment, 43
Politicians, 112, 113, 128
Politicized society, 40–41
Politics, social, 1–11
Pollution, 105, 130, 132, 136
Poor, 69–70
Population, 16, 20
Power, 42, 50, 63. *See also* Coercion, Monopoly power
President, 61–62
Press, 143, 144, 145, 154–55
Prices: increases, 16, 26, 83–85, 89, 136; controls, 36, 89; energy, 87; floors, 133; support system, 133
Primacy of the individual, 52. *See also* Individual freedom
Principles, 8; honesty, 41; justice, 51; equality, 53–54; freedoms as principles, 152–56; constitutional principles for a free economy, 161–68
Private decision making, 21–22, 57
Private markets, 66, 105, 109
Private property, 100–4, 116; rights, 130, 160
Private trade, 22
Production of goods, 129–30
Profit, 66–67. *See also* Free Market
Property rights, 54, 57, 145, 153; distribution, 100; private, 130, 160
Protection: consumer, 29–40; fire, 133–34; police, 133–34
Protesters, 135–37
Public goods, 21, 105, 129, 133–34, 171; quasi, 129, 133
Public interest, 34

R

Rationing system, 89, 90
Rawls, John, 180

Reagan administration, 6
Reckless driving, 35, 131
Redistribution, 17–18, 42. *See also* Distribution
Reform, social, 32
Reformer, social, 9, 25
Regulatory limitations, 166
Relative advantages, 48
Resources, 15, 21, 26, 77, 90, 99, 133
Restrictions on government, *see* Free economy
Revolving simple majority, 165
Risk, 8, 131. *See also* Free market
"Road to serfdom," 58, 122, 172
Roentgen, Wilhelm, 96
Ropke, Wilhelm, 8–9

S

Schlesinger, James, 86, 87
Self-perpetuating government, 131. *See also* Federal government
Shaw, George Bernard, 90
Simon, William E., 4, 40
Skinner, B. F., 49–50, 180
Small government, 23–25, 43, 137
Small groups, 101–2
Smith, Adam, 9, 64–65, 74, 77, 92, 118
Social congestion, 21
Social contract, 160, 180
Social critics, 59; reformers, 9, 25; planners, 56; dictators, 137
Social environment, 9
Socialism, 57
Social politics, 1–11
Social system, 47–48, 68; regulation, 25
Social values, 78, 82, 87, 90
Special interest groups, 22, 62, 110, 118

Specialization, 56
Spillover cost, 129–35 *passim*. *See also* Costs, Externalities
State government, 20–21, 23–24
Stigler, George J., 39, 42; Stigler hypothesis, 169
Supreme Court, 143, 144
Surplus agricultural products, 133

T

Tariff, 36, 117–18
Taxes, 21, 130, 137–38, 162; codes, 21; rates and bases, 24; demands, 28; system, 33; limitations, 162
Taxpayers, 133, 135
Technological external costs, 136
Tornadoes, 134
Tullock, Gordon, 165
"25 and ones," 19
Tyranny, 14, 22, 90, 91; of the majority, 22

U

Unanimous consent, 22, 150
Unemployment, 112, 135
University of North Carolina, 24
Unlimited freedom, 98

Unrestricted government, 33, 117–22 *passim*, 150. *See also* Federal government

V

Vance, Cyrus, 144
Veil of ignorance, 180
Voters, 5–6, 62; median, 106–7
Voting inconsistencies, 110–11
Voting rule, 164–65

W

Wagner, Richard, 127, 164
Washington Post, 144
Waste, 23, 87, 90
Watergate, 152
Wealth, 72; distribution, 69–70; transfers, 70, 167–68. *See also* Distribution
Welfare, 17, 18; wall, 135; tax, 176
Weidenbaum, Murray, 28
Will, George F., 90
Workers, 28, 29
Wortham, Anne, 173
Wriston, Walter B., 5, 151

Y

Yandle, Bruce, 38–39

About the Author

Richard B. McKenzie is Professor of Economics at Clemson University. He received his M.A. from the University of Maryland and his Ph.D. from Virginia Polytechnic Institute and State University.

A syndicated radio commentator on economic issues and an award-winning teacher, he has published numerous scholarly articles on subjects ranging from the economics of education to applied microeconomics. He has authored or co-authored a number of books, including *The New World of Economics: Explorations into the Human Experience*, which has been used since 1975 in over 500 colleges and universities around the world and has been translated into three languages. Other titles are *Modern Political Economy*, *The Political Economy of the Educational Process*, and *Economic Issues in Public Policies*.